Bluejackets on the Elizabeth

Bluejackets on the Elizabeth

A Maritime History of Portsmouth and Norfolk, Virginia
From the Colonial Period to the Present

Alan Flanders

BRANDYLANE PUBLISHERS, INC.

White Stone, Virginia

in cooperation with
the Friends of the Portsmouth Naval Shipyard Museum, Inc.

❋ Brandylane Publishers, Inc.

P.O. Box 261, White Stone, Virginia 22578
(804) 435-6900 or 1 800 553-6922; e-mail: brandy@crosslink.net

Library of Congress Cataloging-in-Publication Data

Flanders, Alan B.
    Bluejackets on the Elizabeth: a maritime history of Portsmouth and
Norfolk, Virginia, from the colonial period to the present / Alan Flanders.
        p.   cm.
    Includes index.
    ISBN 1-883911-30-3
        1. Portsmouth (Va.)—History, Naval.   2.   Norfolk (Va.)—History,
Naval. 3. United States. Navy—History.   I. Title.
F234.P8F53 1998
359.7'09755'52—dc21   98-36966
                                                                                          CIP

This book is dedicated to Mrs. Alice Hanes, curator, director of the Portsmouth Naval Shipyard Museum, *for her steadfast dedication to the preservation of our Navy's history.*

CONTENTS

Preface   *ix*

Sett Sayle for the Southerne Shore   1

Dumore's Revenge   7

A Navy for Virginia   11

Richard Dale: Wanted Dead or Alive   19

Chesapeake   23

Pirates on the Horizon   35

A Dock Brawler Named Farragut   39

Now Boys Are You Ready?   41
The War of 1812 and Craney Island

Tamenend on the Delaware and the God of 2.5   45

Reading, Writing, and Water Wheels   51

History Cut from Granite   55

Chief Black Hawk Smokes the Peace Pipe   59

Gentlemen's Honor and the Nation's Shipyard   61

Around the World from Hampton Roads   67

Fresh Water/Yellow Fever   71

A Duel Between Ironclads   73

Russian Bluebloods and the Columbus Exposition   83

A Steel Cruiser Named Raleigh and a Battleship Called Texas   89

The Wright Brothers and a Moccasin   95

The Jamestown Exposition and a Great White Fleet   97

Hampton Roads Goes Over There   103

Airborne from a Covered Wagon   109

They Came from Shangri-La   113

Dual Hat City   121

A Marriage Built to Last   125

Appendixes   *127*

Index   *143*

PREFACE

Bluejackets on the Elizabeth was written to serve as a companion to Portsmouth historian Marshall Butt's invaluable book, *Portsmouth Under Four Flags*. This author proudly acknowledges the inspiration of Marshall Butt and guidance from Mrs. Alice Hanes, curator, Portsmouth Naval Shipyard Museum.

Having followed Butt's carefully constructed outline of local history, *Bluejackets on the Elizabeth* is an expansion of many maritime events derived from his book. The author has also incorporated much new material that appeared previously in his weekly newspaper column in the *Virginian-Pilot* and other sources.

Considerable treatment is intentionally given to the development of Andrew Sprowle's Gosport shipyard as it evolved into the present Norfolk Naval Shipyard. There is also much attention given to the creation of the Norfolk Naval Base, now the world's largest naval complex, from the former Jamestown Exhibition. Both institutions through a large portion of the twentieth century have been co-dependent, and have thus grown to be of paramount value to the operational needs of the United States Navy and in particular, the U.S. Atlantic Fleet.

Thus, *Bluejackets on the Elizabeth* traces the development of the most powerful navy in world history from its colonial origins on the Elizabeth River to the age of the super carriers, Aegis cruisers, and fast attack nuclear submarines. The author sincerely hopes that this contribution to local maritime history will help bring a broader recognition of the rich naval heritage of the Elizabeth River, and the Bluejackets of Portsmouth and Norfolk.

CHAPTER ONE

Sett Sayle for the Southerne Shore

Portsmouth, Norfolk, and the Navy are forever interwoven in the fabric of American maritime heritage.

Indeed so much naval history has happened since our colonial beginnings along the Elizabeth River, that histories of Portsmouth and Norfolk virtually parallel our evolution into a great maritime nation. In large measure, the ongoing mission of the United States Navy to protect the American concept of freedom of the seas was written along these two common shores that share the Elizabeth.

From the infant days of colonial Virginia to the present, both cities that face one another across this waterfront have been blessed by their location at the southern end of the Chesapeake Bay. Not a single harbor anywhere else in the world has such an enviable position as Portsmouth and Norfolk. Sharing the benefits of the confluence of the Elizabeth and James Rivers to the south and west, the York River and the Chesapeake Bay to the north and the Virginia Capes and the Atlantic Ocean to the east, both cities were coveted by the British, first, and then by the American navy. These natural attributes of deep and protected harbors, which begin at Sewell's Point at Willoughby Spit and stretch all the way up the Elizabeth River to Berkley, the Norfolk Naval Shipyard and beyond, remain as much a drawing card to modern mariners as they did to those English explorers who first made landfall at Cape Henry in 1607. From the beginning, a navy was needed to protect this natural harbor that became Hampton Roads.

1

By his leadership and force of personality, Captain John Smith helped establish the Jamestown settlement some forty miles farther east on the James River. In 1608, he set out on a reconnaissance mission with eleven men in a shallow draft boat to explore the waters around Olde Poynt Comfort (Old Point Comfort). Following a brief excursion down the James, Smith and his party, according to the group's physician, Anthony Bagnall, "sett sayle for the Southerne shore" in the direction of Sewell's Point. Smith and his band of explorers were overwhelmed as they headed up the Elizabeth River. Originally Smith referred to the Elizabeth as the Chesapeake, after the Indian tribe who lived along its banks. Later it was named Elizabeth in honor of Princess Elizabeth Stuart, the eldest daughter of King James I. The colonial explorers were amazed by the concentration of wild game that fled from the noise of their voices, the flocks of water fowl that scurried below their bow and took off to cross the sky overhead, and the schools of fish that rippled the water's surface above rich oyster beds. At first glance, they found more than enough proof that the area could easily support further colonial settlement.

But for these sailors most concerned with the wooden ships that had brought them to Virginia, it was the large stand of uncut forests that caught their attention and stirred their imaginations. Where others might see a large protruding limb or trunk, a seventeenth century shipwright saw a potential spar or mast.

Having used a lead and line to sound the depths as they continued, Smith recorded landfalls and channel boundaries in his log and laboriously corrected his charts. Recognizing the potential of what would become the colonial harbors of Portsmouth and Norfolk, Bagnall wrote, "We sayled up a narrow river up the country of the Chisapeake, it hath a good channell, but many shoules about the entrance." Apparently the native Chisapeakes had long before his arrival established farms along the shore. Bagnall noted: "By that we had sayled six or seaven myles, we saw two or three little garden plots with their houses, the shore overgrowne with the greatest Pyne and Firre trees we ever saw in the Country." Such evidence of fertile land was just the kind of information their sponsors at the Virginia Company in London wanted to hear as they began to advertise the natural attributes of the Elizabeth River.

Early records reveal that in 1620 a shipwright named John Wood "desyred that the Courte would please in regard hee is resolved to inhabite in Virginia, to graunt him 8 Shares in Elizabeth River, for eight Shares of land formerly graunted unto him, because thereon is Timber fittinge for his turne (craft) and water sufficient to Launch such Ships as shal be there built for the use and service of the Company." Wood was not alone; another seafarer, Captain William Tucker, purchased 650 acres at what is today Sewell's Point. Joining these original landowners was shipwright Nicholas Wise, Jr., who became in 1680 the first property owner on the site of what is today downtown Norfolk.

It was no mystery why these early settlers and the many who followed chose the Elizabeth River as an anchorage for the Royal Navy during the next two centuries. The obvious geographical attributes of the area explain why the British navy declared Portsmouth and Norfolk as their "most valuable of Royal ports in all His Majestie's Colonies." Three centuries later, a driver traveling from Little Creek Amphibious Base west to the Norfolk Naval Base and then east again along the waterfront adjacent to the Norfolk Naval Shipyard, the original site of Andrew Sprowle's 1767 Gosport Shipyard, can still see the natural features that first drew the attention of those colonial mariners; an abundance of inlets and bays and adjacent to the shoreline a deep channel.

Anxious to exploit these natural attributes and develop the Colony of Virginia into a rich tobacco plantation, a series of royal governors, in residence at Williamsburg or in England, successfully lobbied the Monarchy during the seventeenth and eighteenth centuries to station British warships on the Elizabeth and in and around Hampton Roads. For nearly a century their mission was to protect an endless stream of convoys that formed in Hampton Roads before entering the Atlantic and beginning their voyage to England. With a steady flow of merchant ships, their holds heavily laden with hogsheads of tobacco, Virginia's Golden Leaf, or with the manufactured goods of Great Britain, Portsmouth and Norfolk's earliest citizens realized their bounty from maritime trade.

It is not surprising, then, that families settled here and developed their skills to serve the fleet or opened businesses related to shipping or the Royal Navy. By the middle of the eighteenth century, both cities boasted a variety of shops, from a rope walk to an instrument maker. A number of craftsmen, including shipwrights, blacksmiths, carpenters, and sailmakers with names like Porter, Grice, Colley, Herbert, Newton, and Eilbeck populated the town's waterfront. Many families, like that of Moses Myers or Andrew Sprowle, grew wealthy by investing in shipping, while others made a comfortable living supplying everything from dry goods to foodstuffs and fresh water to outbound ships. Many of these young men, with the sea in their blood after two generations along the waterfront, hired themselves away as apprentice seamen and pilots, while local young women married officers and crewmen of the Royal Navy and the merchant fleet. As naturally as the ebb and flow of the tides, both cities became major port centers that were married in every way to the sea and the navy.

One of the earliest descriptions of the thriving colonial port of Norfolk comes from the prominent plantation owner and explorer Colonel William Byrd of Westover when he visited in 1728:

> *Norfolk has more the air of a town of any in Virginia. There were then near twenty brigantines and sloops riding at the wharves, and often times they have more. It has all the advantages of situation requisite for trade and navigation. Their trade is chiefly to the West Indies, whither they export abundance of beef, pork, flour and lumber.*

Once these maritime traditions were securely anchored along the shores, no conflict, economic crisis or natural disaster could erase them. In fact, the historical challenges both cities faced because of the sea strengthened their maritime traditions. Under British rule, they produced their share of sailors to fight Spanish and Dutch pirates who operated just off the Virginia coast. However, it was during the Revolutionary War that Portsmouth and Norfolk wedded their future with that of the United States

4

Navy, a tie that has remained unbroken. And so this marriage of convenience in the beginning, has grown into one bound in emotion and family ties that has weathered the storm. Celebrating that love affair is a timeless sea chantey entitled "Norfolk Girls, Portsmouth Maidens" found in Frank Shay's publication, *American Sea Songs and Chanteys.*

"Norfolk Girls, Portsmouth Maidens"

"Our topsails reef'd and filled away,
All snug aloft we know
Despite the storms we'll still be gay
Among our friends below.
Come gather round and listen then,
With spirits warm and true;
Here's a health to all the Norfolk girls,
And Portsmouth maidens too.

"Should the foe appear before us
To our guns we'll fondly cling
While our stars are gleaming o'er us,
Shall their notes of freedom ring.
While life's warm stream is flowing,
Our eager pulses through,
We'll fight for home, the Norfolk girls,
And Portsmouth maidens, too.

"And if we never backward go,
Borne home on ocean's breast,
But find among the caves below
A sailor's place of rest;
Still ere we close our eyes and pass
Beneath the depths of blue,
We'll think of all the Norfolk girls,
And Portsmouth maidens too."

5

CHAPTER TWO

Dunmore's Revenge

*All who were friends to Government, took refuge on
board of the Ships with their whole families, and their
most valuable Effects, some in the Men of War, some
in their own Vessels, others have Chartered such as
were here, so that our Fleet is at present numerous
tho' not powerful. I do assure your Lordship it is a
most melancholy sight to see the numbers of
Gentlemen of very large property with their Ladies
and whole families obliged to betake themselves on
board of Ships, at this season of the year, hardly with
the common necessarys of Life, and great numbers of
poor people without even these, must have perished
had I not been able to supply them with some flour.*

These words written at Norfolk during the winter of 1775
by Virginia's last royal governor, John Murray, Earl of Dunmore,
were but a preamble for the dark days ahead during the winter of
1775-1776.

By the middle of the eighteenth century, the Elizabeth River
waterfront had developed into a vast network of rope walks, saw
mills, warehouses, blacksmith and carpentry shops. Andrew
Sprowle's Gosport shipyard had grown to be one of the most
prosperous in the colonies. The local maritime industry by then
was so sophisticated that it boasted several navigation instrument
repair shops and an apothecary where various mixtures of ship's

paint could be found. Taverns and inns providing British officers and their crew hearty meals and overnight accommodations lined the main streets leading to the Elizabeth. In every way the waterfront traffic of the area resembled exactly what its founders had wished, two bustling port towns patterned after Portsmouth and Gosport, England.

However by January 3, 1776, Norfolk had obviously suffered the most. What had been a prosperous landscape of handsome brick homes, large warehouses, prosperous shops and private shipyards was little more than a heap of ashes and a pile of broken brick and glass.

As small parties of property owners began to return to the waterfront and work their way up the once-busy streets, their minds were filled with confusion and disbelief. On New Year's Day, British ships that offered refuge to Governor Dunmore and his Tory friends, opened fire on colonial militiamen who had taken to sniping against the Royal Navy from nearby warehouses. The Virginians thought they could deny the British landing rights to restock their food and supplies. Dunmore had earlier outraged the locals by seizing the press of a local newspaper and harassing citizens as far as Great Bridge in Norfolk County where he was earlier defeated by the colonials.

Historian H.J. Eckenrode in his 1916 publication, *The Revolution in Virginia,* gives the following account of the burning of Norfolk:

> *The fires begun by balls and landing-parties, spread with great rapidity, because the provincial soldiers, instead of attempting to extinguish them, seized the opportunity to plunder and destroy on their own behalf, determined, as they said, 'to make hay while the sun shines.' Breaking into rum-shops and warehouses, many of them soon became drunk and went in gangs from house to house, smashing in doors, dragging out spoils, and then applying the torch ... The destruction caused by the ships was confined to the waterfront, but the Virginia soldiers involved the whole place in the catastrophe.*

The result was that Norfolk had been destroyed, as it had begun, from the waterfront. Portsmouth's civilian population was for the most part spared from property loss, except for what they had owned in Norfolk. Sprowle's once prosperous Gosport shipyard however was living "on borrowed time."

Even though the majority of the blame was correctly placed on the colonials, the threatening position of the Royal Navy would have a lasting effect on those who came to rebuild. After the destruction of Norfolk, many in the area became early supporters for creating a United States Navy. But first, they would seek their revenge in private boats, equipped with meager weapons but sailed by local sailors of heart and courage. The so-called Virginia Colonial Navy, as fragile a fighting force as it was, firmly established the foundation on which the United States Navy built after the war.

Bypassing the colonial Committees of Correspondence, who saw the need for armed militiamen but overlooked the need for naval defense, the Virginia Convention on June 17, 1776 appointed a Board of Commissioners to "superintend all matters relating to the Navy." Serving on this board were Portsmouth and Norfolk men including Thomas Whiting, John Hutchings, Champion Travis, Thomas Newton, Jr. and George Webb. The ordinance directed this body thus:

> . . . *to superintend and direct the building of all vessels, whether such as are employed for the immediate annoyance of the enemy, or for expediting the transportation of troops over rivers; to manage the outfits of the same, furnish them with necessary ordnance, victualling, provisions, and naval stores; to take under their care the publick rope- walk already erected other rope-walks and dock yards, as occasion may require . . . to provide as large quantities of timber for shipbuilding as to them shall seem fit; . . . to recommend proper persons . . . to fill vacancies in the navy or marines . . . and generally superintend and direct all matters and things to the navy relating . . .*

Local boat builders and merchantmen Thomas Nash, John Herbert and James Maxwell immediately turned out a series of small flat-bottomed boats, "forty feet keel, fourteen feet beam, three feet four inches deep to the top of the gunnell," to transport men and supplies. Another high priority of the commissioners was to rejuvenate construction at Andrew Sprowle's former shipyard at Gosport. Unfortunately, three days after Norfolk was burned, "the Americans in revenge burnt Gosport," which contained "several stone warehouses, miscellaneous storehouses and shops, a large iron crane with brass sheaves, and wharves extending out to deep water." By April 1777, enough equipment and naval stores were gathered there to begin two Continental frigates under the direction of James Maxwell as superintendent, and Paul Loyall, his assistant. Renowned ship constructor David Stodder was brought from Philadelphia to serve as master shipbuilder. Legal title for the Sprowle shipyard property was taken by the state in 1780 with final purchase by the United States government in 1801 for $12,000.

While local shipwrights returned to work, one of the most daring naval conflicts in the Revolutionary War was being played out on the Elizabeth River and Hampton Roads as all Virginia pilots joined the struggle for independence and put their lives, fortunes, and boats on the line of battle. Since they were former officials of the Crown, they knew that immediate execution or life imprisonment awaited them if captured by the British navy. Fortunately for the Virginia Navy, patriotic fervor easily won out, and the familiar pilot boat LIBERTY, and her consorts with the most unlikely names, SALLY and MOLLY, joined in the fray.

CHAPTER THREE

A Navy for Virginia

Governor Thomas Jefferson deserves credit for enlisting the valued services of the pilots by appointing James Barron captain and later commodore of the Virginia Navy. After Barron's brother, Richard, came aboard, the two had little trouble rounding up twenty-four local men to serve in the fledgling fleet of pilot boats and privateers. As each pilot joined, he was commissioned a lieutenant, beginning a tradition that would last in the United States Navy during the War of 1812, the Civil War, and World Wars I and II. Their mission at first was not to engage the enemy so much as obtain vital supplies such as gun powder and grain for the American army then forming under George Washington. As a further inducement for the pilots to stay with the Virginia Navy, the Virginia Assembly approved payment of four shillings per ton for every vessel brought safety to the Elizabeth River.

The pilots knew the odds were against them in the beginning of the war as they could not expect to win every race against the British warships. William Booth, a pilot who made his home here, was given the row galley DRAGON, which drew only nine feet and carried about eighteen three to four-pound cannons. Within weeks of deployment, local pilots were among the earliest casualties of the war.

Private boaters, who knew the channels and how to race their boats from as far as Cape Henry to Portsmouth, were also enlisted. Local pilots like Christopher Morris smuggled war supplies passed the British blockade and served as picket boats that operated with signalmen on shore at key landfalls like Willoughby Spit and Craney Island. While the British fleet was in the bay, Morris would sail down the Elizabeth to Old Point Comfort beach and signal to the Americans not to enter the harbor. From designated areas, the landsmen would either wave a lantern at night or build a bonfire to warn ships that the enemy was near. During daylight masts and pennants were used as warning signals at Craney Island, Old Point Comfort, Little Creek, Lynnhaven, and Cape Henry. Before a British ship spotted them, they would simply lower the mast after removing the pennant and make their escape. Both the lantern and mast and pennant systems proved very effective. The following description of the signal system actually at work was found among Virginia Pilot records in Norfolk.

Pilots stationed their speedy little boats SALLY and MOLLY off Cape Henry as sentinels where they established a crude but effective signal system. A fifty-foot staff erected at Cape Henry served as the initial land signal of approaching enemy vessels. A white flag with a red stripe was hoisted when no enemy was in sight and hauled down the moment a British vessel came within view. During the night a lantern was hoisted on the same pole. A courier was then sent by day or night to Willoughby and from there another mast and signal pennant were used to alert sentries stationed at Craney Island. Couriers were stationed at either point to ride horseback to either Portsmouth or Norfolk with the news that an enemy ship was about to enter the Capes. One of the more dangerous duties of the pilots was to sail out past Cape Henry and search for British warships on the move toward Norfolk. Once they sighted the enemy, they would turn and race toward shore, well ahead of the fleet to signal the lookouts on Cape Henry.

Several serious misadventures befell the Virginians on picket duty during the war, but none surpassed that of Lieutenant Christopher Morris, who chanced upon an abandoned French ship loaded with silkworms and brandy just off shore. Finding no particular value to the silkworms, he proceeded to off-load the kegs of brandy into his boat. Just how much of the cargo he sampled isn't recorded, but within a few hours, he was hailed by a British patrol boat as he entered Hampton Roads apparently without a care in the world.

As the story goes, the good-natured pilot offered his captors, a British officer and two sailors, some of the brandy, whereupon the British sailors and Morris started on another keg. Fortunately, for Morris, the two boats then sailed into a fog bank where he was able to overcome his captors and cut the line to the British boat without being seen. Within minutes, Morris and his inebriated British prisoners and a keg or two less of brandy drifted away from the British fleet. Sober to the fact that he barely missed being placed in the hold of a prison ship and shipped off for England, Morris got his bearings and headed for home. Once he sailed out of the fog bank at the Rip Raps, he headed for Craney Island and then the Elizabeth River. Nearing shore, Morris signaled a lookout and turned over his prisoners to local colonial authorities.

Having enough action for one day, Morris continued toward Gosport where he found a crowd ready to greet him and hear more about his adventure. As folklore has it, they lifted their "hero" off the boat and carried him and the brandy off to a favorite tavern in Portsmouth.

All those who attended the celebration except for Morris remember it as one of the most glorious evenings of the Revolution. It turns out that as his shipmates lifted him from their shoulders he dropped off into a deep sleep. Thinking he was just too tired from his ordeal in combat, his friends carried him into the tavern, propped him up in a corner, and as he snored away, toasted his courage until they reached the dregs of his captured "spoils of war!"

About the same time, the pilot boat MOLLY under the command of a Lieutenant Pasture was able to narrowly escape capture as it slipped through the British blockade off the Capes. The word had reached Williamsburg that the British had posted a small garrison in the West Indies to guard a large supply of gunpowder. Equipped with only two cannons, MOLLY was able to surprise the isolated British and get away with the vital supplies. At night she was off-loaded near Sewell's Point by the colonials and returned to her duties at Cape Henry.

Another daring feat of the Virginia Navy was made by SALLY MORTON under the command of Lieutenant John Cox of Gosport. Governor Patrick Henry ordered pilot Joseph White, along with Cox, to sail her to the French West Indies to pick up a supply of war materials from their French allies. She made several voyages by the British blockade to deliver her cargoes safely to Sewell's Point. However, on a mission south of St. Croix, the schooner was attacked by the British armed ship EAGLE, and, after a bloody struggle, Cox and White were taken prisoner to Tortola.

Locked for months in poorly ventilated prison cells, they suffered under terrible deprivations with diets of bread and water and flea-infested straw for beds. But the two local sailors refused to give any information on future raids.

Their eventual escape reads like movie script. During a work detail, the Americans managed to steal some rope and a grappling hook. At midnight, they tossed the hook over the wall and climbed out. Although sentries opened fire, both managed to jump to safety. After dodging a number of British search parties, they escaped from the island with the help of native boatmen, whom they held at knife-point and finally made their way to St. Eustatia and the American brig RENOWN. Neither of the men saw the shores of the Elizabeth again for nearly four years until they returned in 1780.

Lieutenant John Cox played a major role in another daring mission that year when he led a secret raiding party on Bermuda to capture a large store of gunpowder and munitions. Once again fortune was on his side as he safely delivered it to a landing near Williamsburg in time for Washington's campaign against General Charles (Lord) Cornwallis at Yorktown in October 1781.

Even though a number of Virginia Navy raiding parties from here were highly successful, the casualty rate during the war was high. Approximately one-third of the Virginia colonial pilots were either killed, wounded or imprisoned. Among the thirty-eight men who took commissions in the navy, at least two slaves and one free black man named Cuffee were killed in action aboard the armed schooner WILLIAM GRAVES.

In one incident, ten pilots were sent to their death in 1780 after Governor Thomas Jefferson ordered them to what he thought was the French fleet under Admiral Comte de Grasse. The Virginians cast off under their commander, Captain Richard Barron, to guide the French through the Capes to Sewell's Point planning to capture Cornwallis and his forces as they prepared to depart Portsmouth for Yorktown. However, to the astonishment of the pilots and the consternation of Jefferson, what were supposed to be French ships turned out to be British men-of-war!

Meanwhile the British general moved his troops from Norfolk harbor and their encampment at Portsmouth because he felt the climate unhealthy and the port too difficult to defend. He chose Yorktown because of its easy accessibility to Williamsburg and its strategic value to the rest of Virginia and the Chesapeake. This time the local pilots were more fortunate.

Intelligence reports that the British planned to dig in at Yorktown were gathered by a local spy who happened to be a member of Cornwallis's personal staff. The Virginia Navy relayed all enemy troop movements up and down the Chesapeake Bay so that General Washington could better coordinate local forces as he hurriedly withdrew from New York. The critical challenge to Washington's entire plan to trap Cornwallis at Yorktown was whether the French fleet commanded by the Admiral with the imposing name, Francois Joseph Paul Comte de Grasse, could arrive in time to drive off the British under Admiral Thomas Graves, then anchored at New York.

Governor Jefferson sent a message to Captain Barron to gather the necessary Virginia pilots and get them to the French fleet before it reached the Chesapeake. A single delay, a minor slip in intelligence, and the opportunity would be lost. Although it was argued in local taverns that a similar plan had misfired the year before when the Governor had mistaken a British fleet for the French, Barron had no problem finding the men for the job. Aboard the gallant little armed schooner PATRIOT, they sailed from the Elizabeth River at sunset. It could be said that the fate of American independence sailed with them that night.

After a successful rendezvous at Cape Henry, pilots disguised as fishermen headed far out into the Atlantic in quest of their allies. Finally, one of the schooners reached the French warship CONCORDE. The remaining pilots were dispersed to various units of de Grasse's fleet in the West Indies. With local pilots on board to guide them, the French weighed anchor at Cape Francis, Haiti, and set sail on August 5, 1781, for Virginia.

By August 29, the pilots conned them safely inside Cape Henry, where they were met by a jubilant Captain Barron. When

Admiral Graves arrived from New York, he was astonished to find the French already in position off the Chesapeake and ready to begin what would become known as the Battle of the Capes.

The local men, who spoke little French, had their work cut out for them. After the British were held at bay, French warships had to be moved to the mouth of the York River for blockade duty while Washington pressed his siege lines against Cornwallis.

On September 5, 1781, Admiral Graves was forced to press the attack, but his position was severely weakened by the lack of fresh supplies and water, which had been denied them by the Virginia Navy. At 12:30 P.M., the French fleet weighed anchor off Yorktown and, guided by Portsmouth and Norfolk sailors, entered the Atlantic. It took nearly four hours for both fleets to get into battle positions with the British vanguard firing first. By 6:30 P.M., the battle had ended in a tactical draw, an outstanding victory for Washington's forces.

By September 18, it was all over. The Virginia Navy had come through with the pilots and supplies that contributed to the defeat of one of the greatest military forces in the world. It is significant that sea power played a decisive role in America's first great land victory. Now the question remained whether or not the Americans recognized the full value of building a fleet of their own. Would they have the resolve to build a navy capable of defending their newly earned freedom? Amid the celebrations that broke out across Portsmouth and Norfolk with both church doors and tavern halls sprung wide open, the United States was without a navy and thereby defenseless. Would there now be a repeat of the lawlessness that George Mason described to his son as the British plundered the Virginia shores:

> *Our affairs have been for some time growing from bad to worse. The Enemy's Fleet commands our Rivers, and puts it in their power to remove their Troops from place to place, when, and where they please, without opposition; So that we no sooner collect a Force sufficient to counteract them in one part of the Country, but they shift to another, ravaging, plundering and destroying everything before them.*

At the end of the war, both Portsmouth and Norfolk were devastated. The shipyard at Gosport, where two warships had been started for the Virginia Navy, was decimated. However, what was now lacking in ships, supplies and shipyards was made up by the spirit of local sailors like the Barron brothers and Richard Dale.

CHAPTER FOUR

Richard Dale: Wanted Dead or Alive

Richard Dale, born in 1756, was raised on a plantation in Norfolk County along the Elizabeth River. He was introduced to the waterfront and maritime trade by his shipwright father, Winfield Dale, who died when Richard was ten. Two years later, his mother apprenticed him as a seaman to a Norfolk merchant. In 1776, he joined the newly created Virginia Navy. Hardly had the young seaman recruit settled into his berth before the captain accused Dale of being a Tory who would surrender the vessel.

Dale ended up on a prison ship on the Elizabeth where an old school friend, Josiah Newton, persuaded him to join the British navy. Dale later admitted that at the outbreak of war against Great Britain, his neighbors and close friends demonstrated unwavering support for the British. Wounded after joining a British schooner during a fight with a vessel from the Virginia Navy, Dale was sent to Bermuda Station for recuperation. Upon his return to the Elizabeth River, his vessel, LADY SUSAN, was captured in 1776 and he was imprisoned on the American brig LEXINGTON.

The captain of LEXINGTON recorded in his journal:

> . . . and we tried to talk some sense into our new
> captives, many of whom were Virginians. At least we
> could persuade them to fight for a new nation and not
> just the colony . . . One young gentleman in particular
> seemed properly thoughtful to the alternative, that

being Richard Dale. Upon an oath, he joined our side in the matters.

Now once again on the American side, Dale was on board LEXINGTON when the larger British frigate ALBERT captured the American vessel and for a second time Dale found himself a prisoner of war. Later that night Dale led a band of fellow prisoners onto the deck of LEXINGTON as their British guards had overindulged in rum.

Thereafter, Dale became a target of British propaganda efforts with one article declaring:

The Americans continue to impress and force at gunpoint our most noble gentlemen into the service of their scurvy navy . . . One such young gentleman, recently of Virginia, Richard Dale, was pulled from a British man-of-war and told to serve their foul wishes or die . . . the rebels resort to kidnapping on the high seas. This Dale will attest to if given leave to do so.

Though LEXINGTON had an excellent war record, Dale and his fellow crewmen were captured again by the British months later, and this time Dale was taken to the notorious Mill Prison in Plymouth, England, and placed on a starvation diet. Ever the escape artist, Dale and his fellow inmates began to tunnel under the prison walls, dumping dirt from their pockets into the exercise yard. On February 15, 1777, he and several others escaped.

Dale made it to London only to be arrested by a press gang when he tried to board a merchant ship bound for France. He was subsequently returned to Mill Prison and confined to the infamous "Black Hole." Somehow he bribed an officer of the guard for his uniform and a year later he simply walked out using this clever disguise. This time he successfully made it across the English Channel to Point L'Orient, France and there joined the forces of John Paul Jones. Sizing up the talents of the twenty-one-year old Dale, Jones made him First Lieutenant aboard his ship, BONHOMME RICHARD, which was soon to make history with her sail around Great Britain and the capture of the fifty-gun HMS SERAPIS.

During a vicious night battle on September 23, 1777, when

both ships were lashed together, Lieutenant Dale was BONHOMME RICHARD's second in command and commander of the gun deck. Hearing Jones's famous battle cry, "I have not yet begun to fight," Dale, though seriously wounded, became the first American to board SERAPIS after she struck her colors. Upon their return to France, Jones, Dale and the American crew were national heroes.

Dale's luck faltered during his next duty aboard USS TRUMBULL, and he was subsequently recaptured, this time by a former Norfolk neighbor and friend, Josiah Newton. With their friendship still intact, Newton arranged for Dale to go free during an exchange of prisoners. Before the war ended, Dale's wanted poster read, **WANTED DEAD OR ALIVE,** for spying and impersonating a British officer.

After the war, Richard Dale retired and spent the next decade of his life amassing a small fortune as a private merchant. When the United States Navy was officially recognized in 1794 and Gosport shipyard purchased by the United States government, Dale was made captain and given command of the facility. He ended his career on the banks of the Elizabeth River putting the nation's first official naval shipyard in good order against a tide of isolationism and shrinking budgets.

CHAPTER FIVE

Chesapeake

Even though there was strong evidence that a navy should be created, it would take the combined threats of a war with France, a former ally, and the belligerence of pirates to convince Congress to authorize the construction of six frigates under the Naval Construction Act of 1794. Isolationists made sure that the act contained strict conditions including a statement that read:

. . . if peace shall take place between the United States and the regency of Algiers that no further proceedings be had under this act.

At any rate, the news that one of America's first six frigates would be built at Gosport was literally music to the ears of local shipwrights, carpenters, and blacksmiths. Since the end of the Revolution the yard had remained inactive except for the repair of several privateers and the construction of small gunboats. And even with the existing legislation to build a navy finally on the books, nearly a year would pass before real activity could be seen around the building ways at what has become the Norfolk Naval Shipyard's Trophy Park.

Because of previous destruction by colonial and British forces, lumber and naval stores were at a premium. To get the necessary stock, master shipbuilder John T. Morgan was brought to Gosport from Boston and then sent to Georgia to select timber from choice live oak and red cedar. Through his effort, raw lumber began to fill the "wet slips" around the yard. Just before December 1795, the keel of the new frigate was visible. According to official Navy documents for that year, the keel was completed, and "laid on blocks . . . the stern frame . . . completed and ready for raising." The document also listed "the gun deck and masts, bowsprit, yards and all other spars," ready for completion.

Like pieces of a giant puzzle, the remaining parts of the frigate were arranged beneath the great timber derricks or wooden cranes surrounding the building site. By then local newspapers were announcing the imminent completion of the warship. However, the stroke of a diplomat's pen silenced the axes and stilled the mallets and hammers. The future of not only the frigate, but also the shipyard, Norfolk and Portsmouth had been tossed to the variable winds of international relations. However, the hope of both peacemakers and isolationists were later dashed by a series of illegal boarding and kidnappings of American seamen on the high seas.

After nearly three years of inaction, the issue of freedom of the seas and impressment of American seamen began to capture national attention again. After numerous complaints from that ships flying the United States flag were an open invitation to piracy, Congress passed on April 30, 1798, an act creating the Navy Department. One of the first actions by the Secretary of Navy Benjamin Stoddart was to order Gosport's naval agent, William Pennock, to proceed with construction on the frigate at Gosport.

Once again ship designer and builder Josiah Fox arrived in Portsmouth, this time with a plan to shorten the frigate to 152 feet, 6 inches, allowing a width of 40 feet, 11 inches. At 1,244 tons, the new frigate's armament was reduced from 44 guns to 38. With the bill running to approximately $220,678, the ship was finally ready. A day after the launch on December 2, 1799, the Norfolk *Herald* announced the name of the new frigate as CHESAPEAKE.

So down from Gosport and Norfolk harbor, the United States frigate CHESAPEAKE sailed as one of the nation's original six frigates including UNITED STATES, CONSTELLATION, CONSTITUTION, CONGRESS, and PRESIDENT. All would face challenging seas ahead and all would play major roles in the creation of American sea power. Additionally, they would come to know Gosport, as their home station. CONGRESS would be condemned and broken up here. CHESAPEAKE would be attacked off Cape Henry and cause a war. PRESIDENT would be the flagship of Commodore Richard Dale. UNITED STATES would be sunk in the Elizabeth River. CONSTELLATION would be completely rebuilt at Gosport. And CONSTITUTION would sail from here on a historic voyage around the world!

In the last years of the eighteenth century, Gosport shipyard was not the only center for the revitalization of shipbuilding. On one of America's newest nuclear-powered submarines, SSN NORFOLK, commissioned by the former Secretary of Defense Caspar Weinberger, is a painting of the first ship to bear the name "Norfolk," the brig NORFOLK. Launched in 1798 from the shipyard of Nash and Herbert, the original NORFOLK had a brief but heroic career in action against privateers during the Quasi-War with France. But just how she looked still remains a mystery, except for the following fragmentary notice of her completion in the local newspapers.

The *Norfolk Journal* announced on September 5, 1798:

On Saturday was launched at the Ship Yard of Messrs. Nash and Herbert, Gosport, the United States Brig Norfolk. She is a handsome vessel, is to mount 18 six-pounders, is coppered to her bends, and to be commanded by Captain Thomas Williams . . .

Fortunately a synopsis of her original log survived and gives a brief history of what turned out to be a glorious, albeit, short life of the brig NORFOLK:

. . . Ordered to the West Indies for the purpose of destroying French vessels and protecting American commerce. Under the Command of Master Commandant William Bainbridge, she captured the French privateer VAINQUELRE off Guadaloupe. After valiant service in protection of the American merchant fleet, the Norfolk was sent to Baltimore

25

under the command of Lt. Thomas Calvert and in 1800
her crew was paid off and the Norfolk sold. Her
dimensions being at the time of sale: tonnage—200,
length—140 feet, armament—18 6-pound cannons.

Thus NORFOLK disappeared from history!

But such anonymity was not true of USS CHESAPEAKE. Instead she captured headlines that made her the most controversial of the navy's first ships. While under command of Captain James Barron, she was centermost in the eye of the storm that caused the War of 1812. Later on the field of honor at Bladensburg, Maryland, Captain Barron, while defending his personal honor and the good name of his former ship, took the life of his rival, the popular Stephen Decatur. But before all that notoriety, Barron was already well known along the Elizabeth and throughout the nation as an inventor.

Anybody who has used a washing machine, turned on a bedroom fan, used a metal block and tackle to lift something or admired the giant floating dry docks around Norfolk harbor, should appreciate the genius of Captain James Barron. Besides these inventions, Barron was credited with more than fifteen patents. Among his ideas were plans for a revolutionary steamship and an ironclad warship.

Even though Barron's life story is inseparable from the British warship LEOPARD's attack on USS CHESAPEAKE and his eventual court-martial, his contributions have played a major role in the development of the modern navy.

Barron's new design for a windlass was adopted by the American navy for all its ships in the 1820s. His rope-making machine appeared first on local waterfronts and gradually throughout most of the shipyards of that day. He even invented a cork-cutting machine to keep wines fresh. Perhaps one of his most enduring inventions was the navy's present signal flag code system. But don't look for a ship named after him or any monuments. Instead his name rests securely in nearly six decades of naval history.

Born at Hampton in 1768, he was the youngest son of James Barron, a merchant appointed captain and later commodore of the Virginia Navy during the Revolution. Both James and his brother Samuel interrupted their studies to join their father as midshipmen. Both boys saw action before they finished grammar school.

James Barron went on to earn an appointment as a lieutenant in the United States Navy in 1798. While serving aboard USS UNITED STATES during the Quasi-War with France, he distinguished himself while leading a group of crewmen onto the ship's rigging during a violent storm. Managing to furl the sails, Barron and his crew were credited with saving the ship's masts from breaking. Because of numerous similar acts of courage and leadership, Barron was promoted to captain. In 1800, he became a Norfolk resident and took command of USS WARREN at Gosport. Barron again saw action in the war at Tripoli. During this conflict his shipmate from USS UNITED STATES, Lieutenant Stephen Decatur, became a national hero as well.

On October 31, 1803, USS PHILADELPHIA ran aground off Tripoli in pursuit of a pirate ship. After a futile attempt to raise the ship, Captain William Bainbridge scuttled the forty-gun frigate and surrendered to the pirates. Acting swiftly to deny the pirates their new and awesome advantage, Commodore Edward Preble ordered Decatur to sneak in under the enemy's harbor batteries during the night and sink the captured PHILADELPHIA. Decatur, disguised as a Maltese sailor, took command of the armed ketch INTREPID, and led a band of "Maltese" sailors brandishing tomahawks and swords over the rails of PHILADELPHIA. The Americans were forced to leave their firearms back in the boat less one shot awaken the enemy garrison stationed nearby. After some bitter hand-to-hand combat, all the pirates were either killed or driven overboard.

Combustibles were placed in key areas within PHILADELPHIA. Decatur and his raiding party raced just ahead of the flames and jumped into INTREPID as PHILADELPHIA was engulfed by fire. Miraculously, a mere twenty minutes had been spent for the entire raid without costing a single American life. However, with the light cast from the burning frigate's timbers, enemy forces in Tripoli opened fire with more than one hundred cannons. Several pirate vessels gave chase. Fortune was with the Americans that night off Tripoli as the wind carried INTREPID from the harbor. Just to make sure, Decatur ordered his men to take up their oars after they gave the enemy a defiant cheer.

Midshipman Charles Morris described the scene:

The crew were commenting upon the beauty of the spray thrown up by the shot between us and the brilliant light of the ship rather than calculating any danger that might be apprehended from the contact.

The appearance of the ship was indeed magnificent. The flames in the interior illuminated her ports and, ascending her rigging and masts, formed columns of fire, which meeting the tops, were reflected into beautiful capitals.

The walls of the city and its batteries, and the masts and rigging of cruisers at anchor, brilliantly illuminated and animated by the discharge of artillery, formed worthy adjuncts and appropriate background to the picture.

Thus Decatur's fame was carried by PHILADELPHIA's flames from the "shores of Tripoli" to those of the Elizabeth River and the rest of the nation.

Following an assignment as commanding officer of USS CONSTITUTION, Captain Decatur arrived at Gosport in 1806 as superintendent of ship construction. Apparently he had enough spare time on his hands to court and marry the mayor of Norfolk's daughter, Susan Wheeler. A popular local legend has it that even in his proposal, Decatur told his fiancee that he had already made his vows to his country and that if he were unfaithful to them he would be unworthy of her.

Nineteenth century local school children recited poems that echoed the praises of the nation's greatest hero who lived among them. One such verse, printed in an 1820 grammar book, went: "And proclaim to the world that Columbia is free; beside, my proud trident Decatur shall bear, and the laurels of vict'ry triumphantly wear."

No one can say how far the two rising stars, Barron and Decatur, would have risen had not HMS LEOPARD chosen to stop and search USS CHESAPEAKE off Cape Henry that fateful day in June 1807. But the clouds of war had already gathered with the age-old issue of freedom of the seas at stake. At this time Portsmouth and Norfolk's most famous ship and favorite son were in the eye of the storm.

While on patrol off the Virginia coast on June 21, 1807, British navy Commodore John Erskine Douglas had no choice but to obey his senior, Admiral Berkley, commander in chief of the British navy on the North American station. The orders read:

> *The captains and commanders of his Majesty's ships and vessels under my command, are hereby required and directed in case of meeting with the American frigate CHESAPEAKE, at sea, and without the limits of the United States, to show the captain of her, this order, and to require to search his ship for the deserters . . . and to proceed and search for the same . . .*

Meanwhile, CHESAPEAKE, with Commodore James Barron in command, was heading toward Cape Henry and the Atlantic for a routine patrol. Since the end of the Revolutionary War, the British navy had still maintained a presence in and around Virginia waters and had considered it their right to periodically stop and search American merchantmen. These questionable practices did occasionally produce positive results. However, the interruption of a merchant ship's schedule, sometimes with her crew manhandled, and her cargo plundered, brought emotions to the boiling point locally. Unfortunately local recruiters did not always thoroughly check the background of anxious volunteers, which served to complicate matters even more.

As CHESAPEAKE made her way around Willoughby Spit, no one on board had any idea that they were the subject of a manhunt by the British. Captain Salisbury Pryce Humphreys, however, had other ideas as he readied HMS LEOPARD for general quarters just beyond Cape Henry. It was just before 4 P.M. when LEOPARD's lookout reported CHESAPEAKE sailing in a light breeze between Cape Henry and Cape Charles. At this sighting, the American ship was still within Virginia waters.

Captain Humphreys learned from his lookout that

CHESAPEAKE was not prepared to engage and ordered his ship to come about and pursue the Americans. Having the full advantage, Humphreys then ordered his ship's 50 cannons prepared for action. Meanwhile an American lookout on CHESAPEAKE reported to Commodore Barron that a British man-of-war was closing.

Commodore Barron ordered the lookout to verify that the British ship was indeed LEOPARD, but no further action was taken. At this time British patrol ships routinely patrolled the American coastline from the West Indies to Nova Scotia. London diplomats and British consuls in Norfolk had long promised that the patrols were no real threat to American trade. However, just what the policy was concerning suspected British deserters was about to be learned in a hard and tragic way.

LEOPARD drew within range of the smaller thirty-eight gun CHESAPEAKE and within a few minutes Humphreys sent a dispatch to the Americans. After Commodore Barron read the message, he passed it in disbelief to CHESAPEAKE's master, Captain Gordon. Gordon denied that any deserters from the Royal Navy were on board, and Barron reaffirmed that no British were among the crew. It was at that moment that he noticed gun crews on LEOPARD standing by for action.

After the British messenger left, CHESAPEAKE hurriedly went to general quarters, but it was too late. The first shot from LEOPARD was already on its way, crossing CHESAPEAKE's bow. Four crushing, point-blank range, broadsides followed. Among the torn rigging and splintered deck, three American crewmen lay dead and eighteen fell with serious wounds.

CHESAPEAKE's main deck turned into a madhouse of confusion while the Americans were barely able to get off a single shot. Once again a British search party boarded CHESAPEAKE. This time Barron ordered his flag lowered, and offered his sword and the swords of his officers along with his ship as a prize to Humphreys. He knew that CHESAPEAKE was now in no condition to fight, nor it could it take another series of broadsides. Humphreys, however, refused to accept the swords or the ship. All he wanted were four deserters suspected of hiding among the American crewmen. After CHESAPEAKE's entire crew was mustered, the deserters were found and taken back to LEOPARD.

The British then withdrew, allowing the battered and now disgraced CHESAPEAKE to limp back to Gosport.

As the dead and wounded were ferried to shore, word spread across the town that CHESAPEAKE had been "savagely attacked" by the British. A mob grew around the British consul's residence with hundreds calling for war to be declared. Immediately the Norfolk pilots, to their own financial detriment, declared a strike against all British-flagged merchantmen, while stores and shops refused to buy any British products. As word about the "CHESAPEAKE incident" passed north and south down the coast of the United States, other port cities closed their trade with the British as well. Meanwhile trouble for Commodore Barron brewed aboard CHESAPEAKE as the junior officers of the beaten ship accused their commanding officer of cowardice and premature surrender. The Secretary of the Navy then ordered a Court of Enquiry convened in Norfolk, comprised of Captains Alexander Murray, Isaac Hull, and Isaac Chauncey. Littleton Tazewell, a prominent local attorney and future governor of Virginia, was appointed judge advocate. Their report determined that a court-martial was in order.

By the first of the new year, local hotels and inns filled for what was to be the navy's first national court-martial. At stake were the good names of the "hometown boy," James Barron, and the pride of the navy and the nation. Appointed to find the balance between the two in a military court of law were Captains John Rodger, William Bainbridge, Hugh Campbell, Stephen Decatur and John Shaw. Joining them were masters commandant John Smith, David Porter and Lieutenants Joseph Tarbell, Jacob Jones, James Lawrence and Charles Ludlow.

It was determined that CHESAPEAKE simply was not prepared to fight, and once the battle started, there was such confusion and lack of leadership that any further action by the Americans would have exacted a more terrible toll.

Littleton Tazewell read the verdicts in the tomb-like silence of the captain's quarters. The court determined that Commodore Barron had "neglected the probability of an engagement and had not cleared his ship for action." Furthermore, the court felt that Barron should have detained the British emissary until the decks of CHESAPEAKE were readied. His failure to do so was considered a grave mistake in judgment.

The defeated captain now faced a suspension from navy duty for five years. His old sailing mate and nemesis during the trial, Captain Stephen Decatur, took command of CHESAPEAKE while it was undergoing repairs in the shipyard. From Barron's perspective, the banner of his family had been lowered and now walked upon by a long-standing personal enemy.

For the next twelve years, both Barron and Decatur continued to feud over the incident and the trial. It would take pistols at ten paces on a field of honor to settle matters between them. In their duel at Bladensburg, Maryland, Decatur was killed and Barron seriously wounded. Interwoven throughout the controversy of the CHESAPEAKE-LEOPARD affair was an issue greater than the hatred of two men. Because of the attack on CHESAPEAKE, the American government announced a determined policy to defend the freedom of the seas and the security of all peaceful nations to crew their ships and sail the seas peacefully. This new policy would have profound effects upon the rebuilding of both Portsmouth and Norfolk.

Ironically, just before the War of 1812, the British Admiralty announced the findings of its investigation into the incident. Its report read: "The LEOPARD's attack upon the CHESAPEAKE was an unauthorized act of the officer in command of His Majesty's forces on the coast of America." To help mend harsh feelings, the British government offered a "suitable pecuniary provision for the sufferers in consequence of the attack, including the families of those who fell in action." Furthermore, the British agreed to restore the deck of CHESAPEAKE as close to the original condition as possible.

Those were fair terms when you consider the fate of the deserters. Jenkins Ratford was hanged from the yardarm of HMS HALIFAX, and Ware, Martin and Strachan were sentenced to a series of floggings.

Unfortunately, no apologies could appease the local community, and when hostilities officially broke out between the two nations, USS CHESAPEAKE sailed from Gosport under the command of the former shipyard commandant, Captain Samuel Evans.

This time the area's favorite ship won her pride back as she returned to a hero's welcome after defeating and capturing five British ships, one of which was commanded by CHESAPEAKE's old enemy, Captain Humphreys. In a gesture of good will, Captain Evans allowed Humphreys and his officers to keep their swords in memory of the 1807 incident that had caused the war.

Barron, his name cleared, went on to command the Gosport shipyard. There he designed America's first floating dry dock and presented a written report to the navy department on the advantages of developing ironclad warships. He ended his career as a popular figure in the navy and a beloved hero to the Hampton Roads community and was buried in Trinity Episcopal churchyard, Portsmouth, Virginia on April 21, 1851.

As for CHESAPEAKE, fate still had other things in store. On June 1, 1813, she sailed from Boston under the command of Captain James Lawrence, who had earlier served on the courts-martial of James Barron. Just off the coast, he accepted a challenge from HMS SHANNON. During a furious engagement of broadsides at point-blank range, CHESAPEAKE ensnared her rigging with HMS SHANNON's. The two foes were literally tied to one another during the ensuing battle. During the confusion and fury of combat, CHESAPEAKE, unable to maneuver, was raked by SHANNON's guns. A British marine sighted Lawrence as he urged his crew to beat back SHANNON's raiding party.

Suddenly Lawrence reeled back. The Royal marine made his mark well. Already bleeding from an earlier wound, Lawrence, now gravely wounded, continued to urge his men to fight on. As he was carried below deck, his last orders became his last words and have been a favorite motto of the United States Navy ever since—"Don't give up the ship!"

The Americans responded to their captain's dying wish and fought on until the enemy boarding party overwhelmed those who were left. CHESAPEAKE and the remainder of her crew were taken back to Halifax, Nova Scotia, as a war prize. Her dead including Captain Lawrence and several local sailors were buried near the harbor. The battered hulk that was once the pride of Portsmouth and Norfolk had the inglorious fate of being hauled to Portsmouth, England, where she was broken up. Some of her timbers were taken to the village of Wickham, near Southampton, for construction of a flour mill that is still standing to this day.

CHAPTER SIX

Pirates on the Horizon

During the early years of the nineteenth century, the British navy was not the only threat to maritime trade in these waters. Unfortunately it was an all-too-frequent occurrence for merchant ships to run into the harbor flying distress pennants and passing the word that they had been attacked and looted by pirates!

Gosport became the base for a local and later a national campaign against these seagoing marauders who plagued the merchant trade from the Outer Banks of North Carolina and the Caribbean to the coast of Morocco, Algiers and Tripoli. To combat the likes of daring buccaneers like Edward Teach, better known as Black-beard, and William Kidd, Hampton Roads produced some swashbucklers of its own. And local people built many of the ships that hunted these villains of the high seas and brought them to justice.

As the war against the Barbary pirates in the Mediterranean began to heat up, James Barron was sent to command first USS ESSEX and then USS PRESIDENT in the battle for safer merchant lanes along the coast of Africa. As early as the spring of 1802, USS CHESAPEAKE had been sent into action against the Barbary pirates. Until there was an international consensus, various attempts to eradicate the menace were often fruitless, expensive, and dangerous. One such expedition against the buccaneers of the West Indies brought tragedy to the entire city.

Tiring of renegade bands of deserters from almost every navy in the world raiding American ships, President James Monroe ordered Commodore David W. Porter to Gosport to outfit a squadron for the Caribbean. Broadsheets advertising the need for able-bodied seaman were posted along the city wharves to encourage young local men to join the West Indies-bound squadron.

An article published in the February 10, 1823, edition of the Beacon, a local newspaper, described some of the preparations:

EXPEDITION AGAINST THE PIRATES OF THE WEST INDIES, BEING FITTED OUT AT THE NAVY YARD, COMMODORE DAVID W. PORTER, IN THE USS PEACOCK, COMMANDER.

Four of the small schooners dropped down the Elizabeth River on Thursday, and anchored near the flagship. Yesterday they were joined by the other four schooners, and in the afternoon the SHARK and the store-ship DECOY, were towed down from the yard by the steam galliot [tug] SEA GULL, and all anchored near the PEACOCK.

For young naval officers like Portsmouth's Lieutenant William H. Cocke and others, such a romantic cause was irresistible. He signed on and was soon placed in command of the armed schooner USS FOX.

Next to the 117-foot, 22-gun USS PEACOCK, the eight 31-foot schooners must have seemed like a flock of ducklings swimming around their mother. However these were deadly little ships equipped with three cannon each and built for the kind of swift maneuvering needed to corner the equally swift and small pirate vessels. What would come to be known as the Mosquito Fleet sailed from Gosport on February 14, 1823, bound for the spice islands of the south.

Not until late September, however, did the Mosquito Fleet finally corner and engage the pirates in Funda Bay. Capturing two of the pirate ships and their crews, the fleet destroyed several other enemy ships as well. News of the successful mission normally would have sent both Portsmouth and Norfolk into a frenzy of celebration and merriment had the lamentable event on the schooner USS FOX not occurred.

Ordered to search the harbor of San Juan, Puerto Rico, by Commodore Porter, Cocke sailed his tiny ship beneath the great guns of Moro Castle. Suddenly, without notice or provocation, FOX was fired upon by Spanish positions within the castle. As the crew rushed to battle stations, it was too late. Cocke lay dead on the splintered deck of his schooner. Without reinforcements or orders to engage, FOX hurriedly pulled out of the harbor and returned to the fleet bearing the body of its skipper.

The tragic death of Cocke did not halt Commodore Porter's relentless pursuit of the West Indies pirates as the schooner FOX led the battle against a pirate group operating off the coast of Cuba. She and her sister ships remained on station for nearly three years and made Key West, Florida their base of operations. There they made routine patrols and served as escorts for commercial vessels until the end of the pirate war in 1826. By the mid-nineteenth century, the last pirates captured on the high seas were executed in England.

On July 25, 1832, by an order from the Secretary of the Navy, the remains of Cocke were returned aboard USS PORPOISE and buried in Cedar Grove Cemetery in Portsmouth, Virginia. Inscribed on his tombstone is an epitaph which states, in part: "He was an officer of great merit and bid fair to render essential service to his country, and to reap a harvest of distinguished honor to himself."

CHAPTER SEVEN

A Dock Brawler Named Farragut

The future was very different for another young midshipman, David Glasgow Farragut, who, like Lieutenant Cocke, called Hampton Roads his home and also saw action in the Mosquito Fleet. Unlike Cocke, young Farragut first made his mark in 1811 on the Elizabeth River waterfront as a ten-year old orphan wielding a knife.

Just before the War of 1812, Commodore David Porter's gig became a familiar sight as he made his way across the Elizabeth River from his flagship, USS ESSEX at Gosport. Normally on these trips to the Norfolk waterfront he took his diminutive aide David Farragut. Once the gig was secured at the wharf, Farragut had the boring duty of sitting around until the captain returned. During those long, tedious intervals, he became target of ridicule from the young dock boys. On November 5, 1811, one ruffian poured water on top of the young aide's head to "help him grow some."

The moment Farragut grabbed a boat hook and yanked the prankster down onto the deck, the boat's crew dropped their oars and formed ranks. Led by the bantam Farragut, who now brandished a dagger, they jumped onto the wharf and drove the hecklers down the waterfront, much to the amusement of a crowd of onlookers, including Commodore Porter. Just before a victory could be gained by either side, the constable-on-patrol arrived on the scene and arrested both groups for disturbing the peace.

Delighted at how well the boy had fought, Porter was

overheard to say as he lifted him out of the lock-up: "Well done, Mr. Farragut, you're three pounds of uniform and seventy pounds of fight!" Thus, another local navy legend was born from the incident that heralded a long relationship between the man who would become America's most famous Civil War Admiral and his newly adopted home.

After a distinguished career in the War of 1812, Farragut returned to Gosport in 1821 in time to see the newly built USS DELAWARE begin a new era in warship design. Like any other red-blooded American naval officer, he enjoyed the local social life as well and was a favorite at the dinner parties hosted by shipyard commander Captain Lewis Warrington. At such a soiree a pretty Norfolk girl by the name of Susan Caroline Marchant was seated across the table from him. Soon after Farragut returned from the war against the pirates in the West Indies, the young couple married and began another local-Navy tradition that still has the region referred to [affectionately] as the "Mother-in-Law of the Navy." Lieutenant Farragut rose from a dock brawler in Norfolk to become the admiral who uttered the famous oath at the Battle of Mobile Bay from the deck of his flagship USS HARTFORD: "Damn the torpedoes, full steam ahead!"

For many local residents of that era, Admiral Farragut was always remembered as "three pounds of uniform and seventy pounds of fight!"

CHAPTER EIGHT

Now Boys Are You Ready?
The War of 1812 and Craney Island

During the War of 1812, the Elizabeth River community again was on the front line of action and played a pivotal role in America's second war for independence from Great Britain. As the CHESAPEAKE-LEOPARD incident of 1807 was one of the major causes of the conflict, locals were ardent about settling the score with the British. That score would indeed be settled, but in the most unlikely place-Craney Island-then a nearly deserted stretch of sand and salt marsh jutting towards Hampton Roads from the Elizabeth River.

The war had not gone well for the United States. The local harbor, like most of those along the Atlantic coast, was especially hard hit as British warships operated with little resistance off the Virginia Capes. With impunity they anchored in Hampton Roads to purchase supplies or raid farms for food. By the spring of 1813, one of the bleakest on record for the nation, the British army had defeated the Americans in almost every land engagement. Cities like Washington and Baltimore were terrorized by the enemy. With the exceptions of naval exploits like those of USS CONSTITUTION, the nation was losing the "land" war.

However there were two exceptional successes for the Americans during the war. One was the stunning victory at the Battle of New Orleans. The other was the lesser known but certainly no less dramatic Battle of Craney Island where the British made an amphibious landing to capture Gosport.

41

On June 22, 1813, British troops scrambled down the "Jacob's" ladders from several men-of-war. Commanded by Rear Admiral George Cockburn, they assaulted the shores of Craney Island, with Portsmouth, Gosport and Norfolk as their final targets. Making their landing from barges on the opposite side of the island, an estimated five hundred of the best British regulars deployed into the surf and onto the beach. The British commanders watching from aboard ship were eager to add another quick victory when much to their surprise the tide of battle suddenly turned.

Watching from his inland command post, Captain Arthur Emmerson, commanding officer of a combination of sailors, marines and local militia from USS CONSTELLATION and Fort Norfolk, calmly gave the order. "Now boys, are you ready?" The answer was affirmative. Emmerson then raised his sword as the British landing force fanned out on the open beach and yelled "Fire!"

A Royal marine described the scene later as if "all hell had broken loose" as volley after volley from the American guns tore into their ranks. An army that days before had seemed unstoppable now wavered and halted in the sand as casualties mounted. The American artillery roared back in defiance. Emmerson, moving closer to the British forces, calculated that the enemy would not be able to bring their guns into action because their shells would kill as many of their men as his. Emmerson had guessed correctly; and as his forces advanced to the beach, they were also able to capture all the enemy artillery and supplies that had been landed earlier.

Thinking that the Americans must have superior numbers in the rear to have launched such a brazen advance, the British ordered a hasty retreat. One American rifleman described the retreating foe as "sitting ducks" because they made such easy targets along the open sand and water's edge. Much to his surprise, Emmerson learned later from a prisoner that the landing party had numbered nearly five thousand men-far superior to his own!

As the battle ended with the complete British evacuation, casualty reports listed more than two hundred enemy troops killed, five barges sunk and more than twenty prisoners of war taken along with supplies and munitions. Adding to the American success, about forty British deserters showed up in Portsmouth the following day to surrender. Miraculously, despite the short range artillery duel and close-quarters combat, no Americans were killed.

Cockburn pulled away from Craney Island that night, giving up any chance of future military glory along the Elizabeth.

CHAPTER NINE

Tamenend on the Delaware
and the God of 2.5

Both the Revolutionary War and the War of 1812 slowed the development of Portsmouth and Norfolk into a shipbuilding center. Because many blacksmiths, shipwrights, and sailmakers had left to serve in either the Virginia or the United States Navy, Gosport and the smaller private shipyards suffered. Much of the waterfront lay dormant until the announcement came from the Navy Department in August 1817 that Gosport would be the construction site for the nation's newest ship of the line, the massive three-masted seventy-four gun USS DELAWARE. Every inch a "battleship" of her era, DELAWARE, completed on October 21, 1820, gave the entire area a reason to celebrate.

The *Beacon* wrote that her launching ceremony was planned to be the social event of the decade with following program:

The LAUNCH! Theater will be performed Martin's Comedy, 'Speed the Plough,' a dance of characters after the Comedy 'A visit to London, or Hit at Fashions.' The celebrated 'Shawl Dance,' performed by Miss Clark. National song of Columbia Forever, 'The Glory and Pride of the World.' To which will be added for the first time, a National Operatic piece, written by William Spiller Esq. called the 'Launch.'

Apparently the opera was a hit, opening with a standing-room only crowd even though admission was one dollar for adults and fifty cents for children under twelve. The Beacon previewed the main attraction's nine new songs with maritime titles like "Skyscraper," "Studding Sail," "Junius Brutus Stump," "Grapple," "Ben Block," "Song of the Origin of Gunpowder," "Spritsail," and "Tom Starboard."

The local newspaper also announced the creation of a special duet entitled "Minute Gun at Sea." The remaining resembled a modern day Harborfest:

> *A distant view of the Navy Yard, Bridge and part of Gosport 74. Gun is fired, and the ship glides from the stocks. When she comes to, a broadside will be fired from a frigate. Fire works under the direction of Monsieur Rosainville.*

The event went down in local records as a weekend of almost nonstop celebrations. Throngs numbering in the thousands crowded the banks of the Elizabeth River to revel in a steady wash of bands, parades, concerts and dances. Hotel rooms were booked far in advance as visitors from North Carolina, Washington, Maryland, and even New York arrived in droves. Locals spoke excitedly of a harbor so filled with pleasure boats that one could walk, stem-to-stern, from Norfolk to Portsmouth. The civilian and military communities came together to produce one of the largest parades of sail ever assembled in any era of Hampton Roads history, complete with a display of fireworks. Military units from Richmond joined with local companies as brass bands local dignitaries, and politicians led the way through the city's streets in the type of patriotic splendor usually reserved for the Fourth of July.

As the hour finally approached for the actual launch of USS DELAWARE, the crowd had grown to more than twenty thousand. Every hotel from Norfolk to Suffolk was filled to capacity. But as every festival worker knows, there are always hitches. According to the official program, it had been scheduled for ten o'clock. However, on the morning of October 21, because of the tides, the launch had to be moved ahead one hour. Otherwise the ship's sponsors risked running it aground across the channel from Gosport at St. Helena. Just how officials got a crowd up so early and over to the launch on time presented little challenge according to the *Beacon:*

> *The hour announced for the launching being, necessarily, earlier than met the general convenience, our citizens were aroused from their beds by the bands of the Volunteer Corps, [whose names were obviously left out for their protection!] and before eight o'clock the streets approaching the river were almost impassable, from the numbers anxiously pressing to the steamboats and other conveyances provided to transport them to the favorite scene.*

Three military bands led the burgeoning crowd like a pied piper to the viewing areas around the harbor, continuing to entertain the crowd.

Finally, the blocks were removed from beneath DELAWARE's keel and the giant ship, aided by tallow and grease, began her way with groaning timbers into the Elizabeth. Once the spectators saw that she was afloat, "collations" broke out across the city. Popping champagne corks joined a cacophony of cannon and rifle salutes welcoming the newest warship to the fleet. The celebration continued well past the nine o'clock curfew. Adding to the festivities, DELAWARE's older sister, USS GUERRIERE, flying the flags of most of the nations of the world, illuminated the sky with rockets.

Only a handful of people among the thousands who still celebrated way into that night knew that something had gone wrong. Apparently, the giant DELAWARE had torn away from her restraining cables and grounded on St. Helena. After a survey of the damage, Gosport commander Captain John Cassin reported that the Navy's newest ship was indeed aground and that every sailor and boat in the Elizabeth would be needed to haul her off.

The next day, as the bunting and viewing stands were being torn down, a melancholy little fleet of boats tried to pull DELAWARE free of the mud and sand on the flood tide. Fortunately, a larger fleet of private boatmen witnessed the helpless and embarrassing situation and immediately came to Captain Cassin's aid. By the following day, DELAWARE was secured safely alongside the wharf at Gosport. A grateful Captain Cassin thanked his civilian volunteers for saving his ship and the Navy any further embarrassment.

Nearly three years later, a shipyard repair crew found that DELAWARE had apparently run over some cask and chain used to buoy her restrainers, causing damage to the copper sheathing of her hull. After three summers without this protection, the exposed wood began to rot and finally leak. As the damage was described to Captain Cassin's successor, Captain Lewis Warrington, a novel idea was proposed to remedy the situation. Gosport foreman Charles D. Brodie had drawn up a plan for underwater hull repair. Since there was no dry dock yet to do the repair work and it would take tremendous time and expense to "heave the ship out," Captain Warrington agreed to give Brodie a chance to test his idea.

According to the *Norfolk Herald*:

> *It was in this dilemma that Mr. Brodie suggested the plan of a machine capable of being fitted closely to the ship's side by ropes, calculated to admit both air and light, and having room sufficient for the operation of the workmen who could descend with perfect ease and safety to the keel.*
>
> *No sooner said than done. The machine was forthwith constructed under the direction of Mr. Brodie, and applied to its destined purpose with complete success. The workmen descended with their tools, etc., and commenced their operations: the impaired plank was soon removed and at this moment, they are bolting the new plank, nearly eighteen feet under water, to her side in complete security.*

DELAWARE's hull was successfully repaired and Brodie was publicly acknowledged as the man who saved the ship.

Even though DELAWARE was later burned by the Federals during the evacuation of Gosport at the beginning of the Civil War, a symbolic part of the area's first "battleship" has survived to this day as a beloved monument to the local craftsmen who built her.

Recognized during his time as one of the most talented figurehead sculptors in the nation, William Benson Luke was awarded the contract to carve a figurehead for DELAWARE's bow. Because the Delaware Indian chief Tamenend had befriended William Penn, the Navy Department thought a carving of the chief should grace the bow of DELAWARE. Once finished, Luke's figurehead rode the seas with the warship until her subsequent scuttle and burning. For most of the Civil War, the burned hulk rested on the bottom of the Elizabeth River until the channel was cleared and most of the wreckage removed.

However, like a miracle, Luke's carving of Tamenend survived! Separated from the debris, it was restored at the yard and sent by the commander, Rear Admiral Stephan C. Rowan, to the United States Naval Academy at Annapolis, Maryland. There Luke's work took on a completely unexpected new life.

Remounted in front of Bancroft Hall, the midshipmen's dormitory, the wooden Indian figurehead became a favorite among the students. No one knows exactly why, but soon after Tamenend's arrival, midshipmen began to march in formation past the figurehead on the way to spring final exams. Upon passing the old Chief of the Delaware, each platoon commander would order his men to "left-hand salute." For additional good luck, midshipmen tossed pennies at the statue and performed "snake dances" around its base. Because a midshipman had to get at least a 2.5 grade average to graduate, "Tamenend" soon came to be called the "god of 2.5."

Over the years, Luke's figurehead wore various colors of war paint after pep rallies, and gradually his name was changed to Tecumseh, which has stuck. Fortunately, the figurehead was recognized in 1891 as an artifact and a bronze duplicate has since replaced the weathered original. But Luke's original was saved and after careful restoration, Tamenend now rests in a place of honor at the Naval Academy's Halsey Field House.

CHAPTER TEN

Reading, Writing, and Water Wheels

Shortly after the War of 1812, the Elizabeth became the scene of a major advancement in naval technology. The evolution began as the 1815 arrival of the steamboat WASHINGTON heralded a new era of waterborne transportation. Even though the region would be dominated for the next four decades by both private and military sailing ships, the Elizabeth River became the test site of one of the nation's earliest experiments in steam propulsion. These revolutionary experiments were directed by Lieutenant William H. Hunter. While serving as a midshipman in the 1820s, Hunter had developed a passion for steamships. By the time he had reached the position of naval engineer assigned to Gosport shipyard, steam engines had become a controversial subject within the navy.

In 1840, Hunter persuaded the yard commander, Captain William B. Shubrick, to allow him to supervise the construction of several experimental vessels to determine how paddle-wheelers could be used safely in military vessels. "What I propose," said Hunter, "is the application of fully submerged water-wheels, whether placed horizontally or obliquely, for the purpose of propelling vessels."

The idea shocked the entire naval establishment. For almost 30 years, the nation had grown accustomed to seeing large, half exposed, paddle wheels churning along the side and backs of steam ships. Hunter directed the placement of his newly designed paddle wheels in the following manner:

51

> *My wheels will be placed such that a vessel will float*
> *though the vulnerable parts of the vessel are pierced*
> *or torn by shot. The steam engine, machinery and*
> *water-wheels are placed below a shield deck and*
> *every part of them below the water line, therefore out*
> *of the reach of shot, ram, and torpedo, and the water*
> *wheels, being in their position always submerged, and*
> *relieved from the effect of the sea."*

In 1841, Hunter's GERM was launched in secret for a trial run down the Dismal Swamp Canal. The yard's official report described the operation as "an interesting but unsuccessful experiment in the transition from the orthodox side-wheel to the screw propeller." After making two trial runs in the canal, the GERM was ordered to Washington for further tests.

To the dismay of onlookers GERM briefly reached a top speed of 5 knots. . . . Even though her wheels managed to churn everything into the machinery from mud to moss, Navy officials witnessed the first successful attempt to propel a ship with a totally submerged system. Determined to prove his theory, Hunter designed and built UNION at Gosport in 1842. Even though the Navy finally approved the design, and the patent office accepted Hunter's idea, it would take Swedish inventor John Ericsson's submerged screw propeller to convince the Navy that exposed paddle wheels were a "thing of the past." At any rate, Ericsson gave Hunter real credit for beginning the revolution in warship propulsion at Gosport. As a postscript, Hunter's uniform, still encased in its metal box with some of his official papers, surfaced at a Norfolk costume rental company in 1952. Fortunately, the family who purchased the uniform donated it to the Portsmouth Naval Shipyard Museum in Portsmouth, Virginia, where it is preserved today.

During the first three decades of the nineteenth century, this harbor began to exceed rival ports on the East coast for its concentration of naval vessels. The revitalization of Gosport shipyard led to the area's becoming the operational center of the Atlantic Squadron. As further evidence of how valuable Hampton Roads had become to the Navy Department, an academy for midshipmen training opened at Gosport almost twenty-five years before Annapolis. As early as the fall of 1821, local boys, no older than twelve years old, could present themselves with reference letter in hand to Captain Lewis Warrington, commander at Gosport shipyard. If accepted for an appointment to train as a midshipman, they had three years of rigorous training to earn their commissions. Those young men didn't find ivy-covered brick buildings; instead they were sent directly to the 53-gun frigate USS GUERRIERE, the former flagship of navy legend Captain Stephen Decatur, to quite literally "learn the ropes."

According to an 1821 announcement in the *Beacon*, the training was demanding and strict:

The school will be under the most rigid naval discipline organized on the most efficient plan, and conducted by gentlemen in the naval service well qualified for such duty. [The curriculum included]the different branches necessary for the art of navigation which include arithmetic, both vulgar and decimal, geometry, trigonometry, both plane and spherical, and such other elements of mathematics as are indispensable thereto, and all useful astronomical problems will be taught.

GUERRIERE served for seven years as the Navy's principal training school. Once it was decommissioned and placed in ordinary, the 120-gun USS PENNSYLVANIA took over school duties until the opening of the United States Naval Academy, Annapolis, Maryland, in 1845. However, before the naval academy at Gosport closed, it graduated such legends as David Farragut, Matthew Fontaine Maury, Franklin Buchanan, the first superintendent of Annapolis, Samuel Barron, son of the legendary Commodore James Barron, and John Dahlgren.

CHAPTER ELEVEN

History Cut from Granite

The year 1827 was particularly momentous for Hampton Roads and the navy. Two architectural giants were here to begin two history-making projects. Laomni Baldwin had unrolled his constructor's scroll at Gosport as granite began to arrive for the nation's first dry dock. Just down the Elizabeth River, another renowned architect, John Haviland, revealed his plans for the nation's first permanent (on shore) naval hospital. The plan for a hospital goes back to 1799 when a reluctant Congress passed a bill forcing all seamen to donate twenty cents a month to a national hospital fund. By 1827, political pressure had grown along with the value of the fund so that at last ground could be broken. In March of that year, Secretary of the Navy Samuel Southard, Secretary of War James Barbour, and Commodores Bainbridge, Warrington, and Morris along with Haviland chose the abandoned Fort Nelson on the Elizabeth River as the construction site.

Haviland's plan called for a large hollow square constructed from granite and freestone. The handsome front portion extended 172 feet with a magnificent Doric portico and 10 columns. Twenty granite steps running the whole length of the porch led visitors to the hospital's massive front doors. The building also boasted a fireproof roof of Welsh slate. One of the navy's most famous surgeons, Dr. William P. Williamson, served as advisor during construction. Upon completion in 1830, he opened the wards as chief administrator.

During the height of the area's yellow fever epidemic in

1855, the naval hospital under surgeon Lewis Minor became the operations center for the valiant and costly fight to rid Hampton Roads of this deadly scourge. Minor and his entire staff risked their lives by treating both military and civilian patients. During the Civil War, the hospital was occupied by Confederate forces and treated the wounded from the famous battle between ironclads USS MONITOR and CSS VIRGINIA.

During construction of the naval hospital, one of the most famous events in American naval technological history had commenced at Gosport shipyard. As early as 1825, the Navy Department recognized the need for a granite dry dock. Because of the concentration of navy assets and the geographical advantages of Gosport and Boston, both sites were chosen for construction. In their race to finish first, Gosport shipyard crossed the wire just ahead of Boston's Charlestown shipyard.

Under architect Laomni Baldwin's direction, local lumbermen cut and seasoned whole trees that would serve as part of the original foundation. In short order, the channel that separates Gosport and St. Helena was choked with freshly cut timber. Stone cutters from all over the east coast moved here and awaited the giant granite building blocks to arrive from Massachusetts quarries by barge. Once they arrived, they were chipped to size and finished by skilled masons and given an appearance as one worker said "as being as smooth as bricks and fitting just as tightly."

The project won the attention of the national press, and progress reports with detailed descriptions poured across the United States. The *Norfolk Herald* credited a local engineer as instrumental in the success of the project that began in January 1828 with more than two hundred laborers working relentlessly:

> *The preparatory work of coffer damming, under the superintendence of Henry Singleton is within weeks of completion and this alone, with its appendages and platforms, wharves, etc., will appear to the eyes of the common observer a most stupendous undertaking and of which one unacquainted with the structure of such works can form no idea but from actual observation. Tours of the project will form in Gosport daily.*

One of the most expensive engineering projects of its day, the final cost reached nearly one million dollars. On June 17, 1833, the announcement of America's first dry docking of a naval warship, USS DELAWARE, gave notice to the world of two simultaneous historic events. Gosport shipyard commander Captain Lewis Warrington had the honor to order DELAWARE inside the dry dock. Warrington's chief constructor, Francis Grice, supervised the settling of the giant ship on the wooden blocks below as the dock was pumped dry. Hundreds of spectators crowded the yard and river bank to witness the events and tour boats from County Wharf offered excursions to Dry Dock I for 12 1/2 cents.

Later, as the Civil War construction conversion site of the steam frigate USS MERRIMAC(K) into America's first ironclad CSS VIRGINIA, Dry Dock I soon became known as the "cradle of American naval technology." Much to the credit of those who designed and built it, Dry Dock I remains operational today and is a popular attraction for harbor tour boats.

CHAPTER TWELVE

Chief Black Hawk Smokes the Peace Pipe

With its commanding naval presence and developed waterfront which offered steamship travel up the Chesapeake Bay, the Elizabeth River became a popular destination and stopover for many prominent Americans. But it took a presidential order from Andrew Jackson to get Indian Chief Black Hawk and his son off the war path for a visit in 1833.

President Jackson had written, "The only way you could whip the Indians who were tormenting the western settlers was to overwhelm them with superior forces and put them on the right path to glory." Having just completed a visit to Gosport shipyard himself, Jackson thought that Black Hawk would be impressed by the might of the American navy anchored along the Elizabeth, so he ordered him removed from captivity at Fort Monroe. Jackson further hoped that once Black Hawk took a specially planned harbor tour, the Indian warrior might "see the number and power of our people, that they may go home and counsel their young men against taking up the hatchet in future, when there is no sort of hope of accomplishing anything by it, but their own complete destruction."

Defiant to the end, however, Black Hawk warned his escorts that once he was in the boat crossing the great lake, he would cast a spell on his captors and escape with ease. Naval officers cautioned that if he tried anything, they would pull the plug on the barge and sink the entire group. Needless to say, their journey across Hampton Roads was uneventful since neither Black Hawk nor his son could swim.

The tour around the local waterfront with its impressive array of warships seemed to have no impact until they reached USS DELAWARE readying to enter Dry Dock I. Visibly shaken as he stared at the ship's impressive battery of cannons, Black Hawk asked in an awestruck voice, "May I be shown the man who made this great canoe, that I may take him by the hand and pay him respects."

On the way back to Fort Monroe, the humbled warriors glimpsed DELAWARE's bow figure, Tamenend, and recognizing the likeness as an Indian warrior, Black Hawk stood erect in the boat and gave a war whoop. A Marine guard on the boat grabbed for his rifle, but there was no need; Black Hawk had just been overwhelmed that the "great canoe" not only had an Indian name, but an Indian spirit on the bow! It was time for Black Hawk to throw down the tomahawk and pick up the peace pipe.

CHAPTER THIRTEEN

Gentlemen's Honor
and the Nation's Shipyard

Along with the construction of USS DELAWARE, the nation's first naval hospital, and dry dock, and the choice of Gosport as the operational center for the Atlantic Squadron, Gosport shipyard during the 1830s was well on its way to becoming the nation's preeminent government repair facility.

As mentioned earlier the yard was purchased by the federal government from the Commonwealth of Virginia in 1801. The deed conveying approximately sixteen acres to the United States for twelve thousand dollars was executed on June 15 of that year by Governor James Monroe. This original tract was situated on the northeast corner of the present Norfolk Naval Shipyard at what is now known as Trophy Park. Archival records state that prior to 1827, the following structures had been completed along the waterfront: a granite building ways, an office, a commandant's house, marine barracks, a brick storehouse (which stood near the present First Street Gate), a powder magazine, a blacksmith shop, and two large covered buildings known as ship-houses.

A large, frame two-story building used as the first marine hospital was located in the center of the tract. Adjacent to the hospital was a rigging loft and gunner's store room or armory. A brick wall begun in 1803, (part of which is still standing complete with sentry ports), marked the northern and western boundaries. A number of wooden docks and wharves covered the waterfront along with a rope walk and smaller shops housing carpentry work spaces and paint stores. United States Marines were attached to Gosport as early as October 1801, detached in 1804, and reestablished in November 1807, making it the second oldest Marine garrison in the nation until final disestablishment on 20 September 1978.

Although the early nineteenth century looks on the surface to be one of quiet growth and social stability for this area's naval history, Saturday mornings were frequently interrupted by pistol shots "at ten paces" as young midshipmen, following the fashion of the day, settled their differences by dueling! One of many such incidents began on the deck of USS CONSTELLATION as she made her way into Hampton Roads in 1825.

The conversation between midshipmen Charles F. Shoemaker and Thomas S. Wayne began pleasantly enough as both were looking forward to arriving here in time for the fall debutante season. The two young bachelors naturally turned the conversation to the young ladies they hoped to escort to the cotillion. Before the weekend was over, neither would be attending the dance; instead the crew of CONSTELLATION would be listening to the last rites for Midshipman Shoemaker.

Witnesses later testified at an official inquiry that Shoemaker and Wayne had been the closest of friends until Midshipman Shoemaker "got rather free with his words and made some disparaging remarks about a certain young lady from one of the city's leading families." As the conversation continued, Wayne realized that the subject of Shoemaker's vile remarks was in fact the young lady he hoped to escort. Making matters worse, they both learned that she had invited both young gentlemen to escort her.

As a result, Midshipman Wayne called Midshipman Shoemaker to duel on point of honor concerning the now severely impugned reputation of the young lady in question.

Before CONSTELLATION anchored off Fort Norfolk, seconds or close friends of both midshipmen exchanged the personal cards of the two former friends and the time and location of the duel was set. The open fields adjacent to old Fort Nelson across the Elizabeth River had already been recognized as a designated area to settle such affairs and as both men were agreeable, arrangements were made to row both of them at daybreak the following day to what had become the Navy's "field of honor."

At dawn, the retort of two pistol shots reverberated down the river. In front of their seconds and official witnesses, one midshipmen fell mortally wounded on the wet grass. His victorious opponent, according to form, handed his pistol to his second, and walked slowly over to his fallen shipmate to accept a formal apology. Meanwhile CONSTELLATION's entire crew stood anxiously on deck straining their eyes to see which midshipman would walk from the morning mists at Fort Nelson. There were no cheers nor rebukes as Midshipman Wayne and his escorts shoved off with the body of Shoemaker from the shore.

Due to the prevalence of dueling in that era, justice was swift. A county jury acquitted Midshipman Wayne, as did the military board of inquiry. The honor of the young lady in question had been preserved.

A similar tragedy occurred in March 1826 within Gosport shipyard itself. The *Norfolk Herald* reported the details that brought two United States Marine Corps officers to their own "field of honor":

Between Lieutenants William T. Bourne and Constantine Smith, a feud had for some time existed, originating from some bickering upon points of duty, which would have resulted in a duel in the early stages had it not been for the prompt attention of their commanding officer Major Anderson.

But even the restraining influence of superiors was not enough to quench the hatred between the two young men in question. To keep them apart according to the *Herald:*

Orders were therefore given to the guards to report to Major Anderson every suspicious movement of the misguided officers. Accordingly, on Saturday morning last, shortly after daybreak, the sergeant of the guard reported to Captain Linton, the officer on duty, that Lieutenants Smith and Bourne were seen a few minutes before to leave the barracks together, upon which

*Captain Linton ordered him to take a file of men and go
in quest of them across the footbridge. At the same time
he despatched scouts in other directions with orders to
return the absentees immediately to their quarters.*

Fanning out in all directions for over a quarter of a mile, the
search party was unable to get to the two men in time. Suddenly
the sound of two pistol shots ripped across Gosport. Following
the direction of the reports as best they could, the marines came
upon Lieutenant Bourne lying on his back with blood still flowing
from a wound in his side. Standing over him, smoking pistol still
in hand, was a speechless Lieutenant Smith. In a state of shock,
Smith went through the almost hypnotic motion of reaching down
besides Bourne, picking up his pistol, and handing them both
over to the sergeant of the guard. Still in a dream-state, Smith
slowly turned away and led the search party that bore the dying
Lieutenant Bourne back to the barracks in total silence. There he
was placed on his bed with Lieutenant Smith still standing by. In
an hour, Lieutenant Bourne was dead. Following his testimony
at a board of inquiry, Smith fled from his barracks that night on a
packet boat for New York.

According to the *Herald* report, "It is the general belief that
they fought without seconds; but the sergeant in his testimony
before the inquest stated that he saw two men as they came up,
hurrying away through the bushes, and soon heard the rattling of
carriage wheels. We understand that Lieutenant Bourne was the
challenger and that Smith confessed that they fought at *two paces
distance!*"

An article followed three years later in the Herald on
September 25, 1829 which closed the entire matter:

*Lieutenant Constantine Smith of the Marine Corps,
charged with the death of the late Lieutenant Bourne,
of the same corps in a duel, has been tried at the
present session of the Superior Court of Law of Norfolk
County, and unanimously acquitted by the verdict of
a most intelligent jury.*

And there the matter was literally laid to rest. Despite such stories of the so-called "swashbuckling" days of yore, both Portsmouth and Norfolk were by the mid-nineteenth century national maritime centers that were increasingly leaning toward industrialization.

CHAPTER FOURTEEN

Around the World from Hampton Roads

Coupled with the continued development of Gosport was the growth of smaller shipyards and related industries along the southern branch of the Elizabeth River. By 1850, the lists of privately owned yards included names like Thomas, Nash, Porter, Dyson, Page and Allen, which competed with the larger Gosport facility for government and private contracts during this period. Associated iron works like Eagle, Atlantic, Mahaffey's, and Green's also helped turned the Norfolk and Portsmouth waterfronts into an industrial Mecca. Steam power, no longer a rarity, was running machinery in the smaller yards and sawmills. Ship propulsion systems were now also commonly run by steam, even though the number of wooden-masted sailboats and ships in the Elizabeth River far outnumbered their coal-burning counterparts. Because of the development of its harbor and substantial supporting industries, Gosport shipyard was often the staging area and point of embarkation for many of the nation's most important naval expeditions. Two of them, the Wilkes Expedition to Antarctica and the Perry Voyage to Japan, had profound effects on the nation's scientific and economic development. The third, a circumnavigation of the world by Old Ironsides, helped serve notice to the world of America's arrival as a preeminent naval power. All three voyages began of course with significant fanfare.

On July 26, 1838, Hampton Roads was full of excitement in anticipation of her first presidential visit. Besides the crowds of local notables who booked hotels on both sides of the river to see Martin Van Buren, dozens of the nation's foremost scientists and naturalists also took rooms wherever available. Instead of pursuing political futures like the vast majority of visitors, they came to make last minute suggestions and contributions to the National Expedition to the Southern Ocean (Antarctica). Under the direction of Commander Charles Wilkes, the expedition had been forming at Gosport for the last three years.

The expedition's flagship, USS MACEDONIA, and her consort, USS PIONEER, were built here especially for the voyage, but were reassigned just prior to setting sail. However, the area's financial investment in the voyage was recouped by the government's assignment of another flagship, USS VINCENNES, along with support vessels USS PEACOCK, PORPOISE, FLYING FISH, OREGON and RELIEF outfitted here as well. After a successful voyage to the Antarctica, Wilkes was honored by having a sizable chunk of the most southern subcontinent named after him, Wilkes Land. Many natural species he gathered became the nucleus for the great collection of the Smithsonian Institution.

One of the most colorful naval officers of his time, Captain John "Madjack" Percival called Gosport his home in the fall of 1843. There he was in charge of having the legendary frigate USS CONSTITUTION, overhauled here for a two and one-half years' flag-showing voyage around the world. During the voyage, American navigators were assigned to correct their charts for the coast of Africa. They also charted for the first time with accuracy the island of Madagascar. Another assignment tasked them to take copious intelligence reports on foreign military posts wherever they observed them. During the voyage, the chief naturalist from Philadelphia, Dr. Joseph Cooper Rhinehart, conducted some of the first experiments to determine the cause of yellow fever.

It was also on this voyage that Captain Percival learned that Cochin China's (now Vietnam) French Bishop had been taken prisoner and held for ransom. While anchored at Turon, Percival led America's first expeditionary force into Cochin China to force the freedom of the Frenchman that he was able to achieve after several fierce battles with local rebels. Before returning,

CONSTITUTION sailed for the California coast and joined American naval forces in the Mexican War. Fortunately, the ship's carpenter, Henry George Thomas of Norfolk, kept an extensive personal account of the voyage in his journal that has been handed down through the generations and preserved by his direct descendants.

Perhaps no other single voyage in American history has had such a continued effect on our nation's development as that of the United States Navy's voyage to open Japan in 1852. Under the command of Commodore Matthew Galbraith Perry, brother of the War of 1812 naval hero Oliver Hazard Perry, an entire fleet of warships including USS MISSISSIPPI, POWHATAN, SUSQUEHANNA, VERMONT, PRINCETON, ALLEGHENY, SARATOGA, PLYMOUTH, VINCENNES, MACEDONIAN and PORPOISE was made ready for action. Under orders from President Millard Fillmore, Commodore Perry was tasked with "opening the door of trade with Japan" to American merchantmen as they already were to other foreign trading partners.

Burdened with diplomatic gifts, many with local origins including a miniature steam locomotive for the emperor, Perry's expedition finally made Yedo Bay, Tokyo on July 8, 1853. After nearly two years of presentations and official diplomatic parleys, Perry returned here in 1855 bearing gifts from the Japanese royal family for the president and a series of trade agreements inked and signed.

CHAPTER FIFTEEN

Fresh Water/Yellow Fever

While local Navy ships were carrying the flag to the four corners of the globe, local marine scientists and technicians continued to make history on the Elizabeth River.

An experiment aboard the steamer USS SARANAC to convert salt water into fresh was announced from Gosport shipyard on December 16, 1851. A correspondent from the Norfolk *Beacon* described the implications of the experiment:

> *It was long considered impossible to render sea water drinkable because of the Bromine that remained in it. This could produce a bitter taste and nausea. The experiment however has at last resulted satisfactorily, and the distilled water, after it is cooled, is said to be as good as any water in the world. We believe the same SARANAC is the only steamer to which this valuable invention has been applied.*

Like a harbinger of things to come as Hampton Roads would become the scene for the world's first two battle-tested ironclads, an experiment to test the vulnerability of iron ships to shot was conducted here in April 1852. President Franklin Pierce and his cabinet looked on at an event that would spell the end of wooden warships.

According to an eyewitness account, "For some time past the iron steamer WATER WITCH has been the subject of the various experiments in testing the fitness of iron vessels for purposes of war, during which she has been considerably battered; but the result of the firing yesterday proved that iron is not so invulnerable as many heretofore supposed."

In 1855, Norfolk and Portsmouth craftsmen were given the job of conducting a full inspection of USS CONSTITUTION's sister ship, USS CONSTELLATION. Special attention was placed on the old warrior's timbers. After a thorough examination, they were found to be totally rotten. But instead of condemning her to a slow death in "rotten row," orders were sent from Washington to completely disassemble her. Even though just a few of her original timbers were salvageable, her lines were redrawn by local ship constructor John L. Porter, converting her from the original frigate design to a twenty-two-gun sloop-of-war. Thus the argument goes that the popular tourist attraction in Baltimore's Inner Harbor is a later Gosport remake of the original CONSTELLATION.

Unfortunately, as mentioned earlier, neither Norfolk nor Portsmouth was able to deal with the terrible scourge of the yellow fever epidemic that broke out from the harbor that year and devastated thousands. The origin of the pestilence was traced to the merchant ship BEN FRANKLIN that docked at the Page and Allen Shipyard, Gosport. The ship was not properly inspected nor was it conducted through quarantine correctly and mosquitoes carrying the dreaded disease escaped to spread down the Elizabeth River and deep into both cities. Navy officials at the naval hospital, on ship, and in the yard risked their lives to help comfort the thousands who were stricken. Helpless to stem the tide of death and illness, many fled inland, while the rest were forced to wait until colder temperatures in the fall and winter killed the infected mosquitoes. Particularly hard hit during the outbreak were hundreds of Irish immigrants who had settled in tenements along the Gosport waterfront in an area known as Irish or Shanty Row. Because of the extreme loss of life there, all naval facilities including the shipyard were closed.

CHAPTER SIXTEEN

A Duel Between Ironclads

Less than five years after the ship-borne devastation of yellow fever, the Elizabeth was in the bull's eye of another deadly drama-the outbreak of the Civil War. Even though local representatives to the Richmond Convention voted against the call for secession, Virginia joined her southern neighbors in June 1861 and become part of the Confederacy. Determined that all Federal property would be protected, troops were reinforced at nearby Fort Monroe and armed sentries posted at the Gosport shipyard.

Conditions were now ripe for war in Hampton Roads. Before Virginia's secession was finally approved, locals donned the gray uniforms of Virginia militiamen and swore their allegiance to Richmond rather than to the new Confederate States of America. Meanwhile, there were enough Navy ships in the harbor to destroy most of Norfolk and Portsmouth. Hundreds of cannons bristled from the wooden hulls of USS PENNSYLVANIA, COLUMBUS, DELAWARE, NEW YORK, MERRIMAC(K), UNITED STATES, COLUMBIA, RARITAN, PLYMOUTH, GERMANTOWN, DOLPHIN AND CUMBERLAND. Even the tremendous firepower of these assembled warships was not enough to stem the tide of rebel fervor that quickly spread by the night of April 20, 1861, to the Gosport gate. Before that evening was over, the Navy was to suffer its greatest loss in ships and material until the Japanese attack on Pearl Harbor eighty years later.

From official accounts examined later to determine whether to bring charges against Gosport Commanding Officer Captain

73

Charles S. McCauley, it was decided that the administration of the yard was put in a position of hysteria by orchestrated rumors of a planned rebel attack. Misinterpreting the intention of politically sensitive orders from Washington that were designed to avoid an armed incident in Virginia rather than force the Old Dominion in the Confederacy, McCauley did not fully prepare the yard's garrison or its ships to resist attack. Instead, Captain McCauley panicked and ordered the shipyard and warships there burned and scuttled. Before daybreak on April 21, the American flag was lowered, and Captain McCauley and his officers and men boarded USS PAWNEE for their escape to Fort Monroe, illuminated down river by the still-burning yard and ships.

The next day, Virginia forces under the command of Captain Robert Pegram raised their flag over the charred remains of giant ship houses and other rubble that had been one of the most advanced shipyards and naval stations in the nation. Fortunately for the Confederates under Commodore French Forrest, who would officially occupy the harbor on April 22, the dry dock was left intact along with 1,085 cannons and stores of ordnance and various marine supplies.

It was soon determined that Gosport had more than enough ordnance to share with surrounding Confederate batteries. Hundreds of former United States naval cannons and equipment were shipped as far as the Outer Banks of North Carolina, Craney Island, Sewell's Point and to the upper reaches of the James River at Drewry's Bluff. During the first several months of rebel occupation, Gosport became the Confederate Navy's major supply station as lumber, rope, and rigging were sent to shipyards throughout the South. Hoping to put a quick stop to these shipments, the Union navy tightened the blockade around Hampton Roads off the Virginia Capes. Meanwhile, Federal warships like USS CUMBERLAND, CONGRESS and MINNESOTA took positions off Newport News point, just south of Fort Monroe to further curtail rebel shipments. For a third time, both Portsmouth and Norfolk were cities under siege from the sea.

However, the real damage had already been done. Because of the hasty and disorganized Federal withdrawal from Norfolk, invaluable equipment had already found its way into Confederate hands. By late spring, Confederate naval officials, including ship constructor John L. Porter and steam engineer William P. Williamson, both of Portsmouth, were busy examining the burned hull of the steam frigate USS MERRIMAC(K) for conversion into an ironclad warship. Porter described this exact moment in his memoir, written just after the war:

> *We had the hulk of the MERRIMAC* [Porter always left the "K" off end of the name], *which the Federals had burned to the water's edge, brought into the dry dock. I realized early the great advantage the North would have with its Navy, so I made a model for an ironclad bomb-proof similar to the one I had made in Pittsburgh [shipyard] in 1846 and submitted it to Mallory in Richmond.*

Since time was against them, the Confederates had Baker Brothers Salvage Company of Norfolk pump out the burned hulk of MERRIMAC(K) and position it in Gosport shipyard's Dry Dock I. Porter continues:

> *I commenced to cutting her down on a straight line from forward to aft. I had to submerge the hull two feet under water for protection. Despite what others may say, I was never able to completely finish her below the water line. The shield above the water line was her only shell proof section.*

As iron plating rolled into Norfolk by rail from Tredegar Iron Works in Richmond, all the local privately owned shipyards joined forces to keep the effort going throughout the remainder of 1861. Fortunately for the Confederates, a large supply of gunpowder and ordnance had been captured at Fort Norfolk and was later loaded aboard the ironclad's magazine.

By March 1862, journalists from Europe and most of the United States had sailed here to visit the conversion site. As news reached Washington that the Confederates had MERRIMAC(K) in dry dock and were working feverishly to turn her into an ironclad, President Lincoln ordered the United States

Navy to produce an ironclad of their own at once. This time fortune smiled upon the North as Swedish-born inventor John Ericsson submitted his novel drawing of a large, iron-plated turret carrying two cannons to be mounted on a shallow-draft boat. It was roughly half the size of Porter's 275-foot long ironclad.

History records that onlookers for the most part ridiculed both projects, calling Porter's ironclad a "floating coffin," and Ericsson's MONITOR a "cheese box on a raft." However, once the stage was set for them to fight in Hampton Roads in March 1862, both would prove wooden-hulled warships obsolete.

Even though Ericsson raced for completion of his ship at Greenpoint, New York, Porter got his ironclad out of the dry dock first. She was christened CSS VIRGINIA. Under pressure from Richmond to use VIRGINIA to smash the ever tightening blockade around the harbor, Porter was disappointed that his ship was launched prematurely. He wrote:

Even though the ship mounted eight 9-inch shell guns in the broadside and two rifled pivot guns on the bow and stern, four of the quarter ports had no guns in them. I had the ports fastened shut with iron during the battle, and as it was difficult to maneuver the MERRIMAC, she was at a constant disadvantage for this.

Equipped with only exploding shells, not solid shot, propelled by a faulty auxiliary engine which had already been condemned by United States Navy authorities, affixed with an iron ram that had been improperly added at the last minute and with a turning radius that took at least one-half hour, CSS VIRGINIA steamed from Gosport on March 8, 1862. Steaming along at the ponderous speed of less than eight knots, with her smaller consorts, the armed tugs RALEIGH and BEAUFORT at her sides, she took the cheers of hundreds of well-wishers who lined both sides of the Elizabeth River. At the Federal anchorage off Newport News, no one aboard USS CUMBERLAND, CONGRESS, ROANOKE, ST. LAWRENCE or MINNESOTA expected much action that Saturday afternoon. Lookouts spotted a strange craft billowing a large plume of black smoke off to the east, but neither officers nor men could determine its origin.

Once CSS VIRGINIA was clearly in sight with her captain, Commodore Franklin Buchanan, the first superintendent of the United States Naval Academy, standing half-exposed to fire from her forward hatchway, there was little time to sound the alarm and prepare for battle. Reaching top speed, VIRGINIA passed by both CUMBERLAND and CONGRESS as shot from both ships bounced harmlessly from her iron-plated sides. Having turned up stream, VIRGINIA then made a full turn and came crashing, ram first, into the wooden sides of CUMBERLAND. As CUMBERLAND's timbers broke beneath the water line, and the screaming sound of drowning men filled the ship, there was little her crew could do. CUMBERLAND began to fill with water as VIRGINIA reversed engines to extract herself from the crushed ribs of her victim. But suddenly the Confederate ironclad's engine stalled. Now the panic of certain death spread from one ship to the other. Repeatedly engineers aboard VIRGINIA tried to bring her machinery to life.

At that moment there was a coughing sound below in the Virginia's engine room as the tremendous weight of the sinking CUMBERLAND broke off the stem of the ram with a loud crack. VIRGINIA was free as billows of black coal smoke poured from her stack and blanketed the scene from the view of the CONGRESS. Meanwhile, MINNESOTA, ST. LAWRENCE and ROANOKE had raised their anchors and in a panic raced for safety only to ground themselves on a nearby Hampton sand bar. From their embarrassing position, they waited the outcome, firing whenever VIRGINIA came into view.

With a deadly confidence, VIRGINIA was able to move slowly toward another victim, as shot according to one crewmen "bounced off her iron-plated roof like hail."

With CUMBERLAND all but sunk and hundreds of her crewmen desperately trying to save themselves, VIRGINIA sailed ominously close to the wooden hull of CONGRESS. After receiving more direct fire, she delivered her own salvo into the Union ship. Within moments, part of CONGRESS's battery was torn to shreds as the decks of the great warship literally ran red with blood. Fire broke out below CONGRESS's decks after another broadside from VIRGINIA. Then orders were given to strike her colors and abandon ship lest the magazine blow. Seeing clearly the growing catastrophe aboard both CUMBERLAND and CONGRESS, Commodore Buchanan ordered a flag of truce raised aboard VIRGINIA so that his Confederate crew might rescue drowning Federal sailors. Just after the rescue operation started, a marine still in the rigging of CONGRESS drew an accurate bead on Buchanan, sending him below VIRGINIA's deck with a serious wound. At once Executive Officer Catesby A. P. Jones took command and ordered the truce flag lowered. The battle resumed, resulting in scores being killed board CONGRESS and CUMBERLAND. Seeing the fate of her sister ships, MINNESOTA, now stranded on a sandbar prepared for the worst. Fortunately the day had grown too long for VIRGINIA. Not only had her commanding officer been taken out of action, but coal reserves were slight and ammunition low. Furthermore, her chief pilot Hezekiah Williams noted that as her fuel and ammunition were used up, VIRGINIA rose in the water, exposing wooden hull sections that had previously been hidden below the water line. It was therefore sound judgment on Captain Jones's part to withdraw VIRGINIA back to her anchorage at Norfolk to load more coal and fresh ammunition. A small but steady leak had sprung around VIRGINIA's caulking near the broken bow stem that once held the ram. The ram was now lodged into the side of the sunken CUMBERLAND like a giant iron thorn.

Despite a few broken iron plates, a minor leak, faulty engines, and the wounding of Buchanan, there was no doubt on either side who changed the course of naval history that fateful day in March. As terrible and bloody as the fighting had been, many on both sides lamented the somewhat easy victory VIRGINIA had given the Confederacy. During the first day's battle, the romantic era of "iron men and wooden ships" had ended forever. Now both sides of Hampton Roads waited for VIRGINIA to return the next day and finish off her third victim, the helpless MINNESOTA.

However, VIRGINIA would be forced to share the stage of naval history on March 9, 1862. The storm-tossed USS MONITOR, arrived just in time to witness the magazine of CONGRESS explode. As the last remnants of CONGRESS burned slowly to the water line, MONITOR steamed around to MINNESOTA and took up a defensive position just behind the giant ship. The sun broke that morning on March 9, 1862 as a curtain rising on the second act of one of the world's most important naval dramas. Although the event would come to be called the Battle of Hampton Roads, it would forever be remembered in history as "The Battle Between the MONITOR and MERRIMAC(K)."

Meanwhile, news of the first day's battle ricocheted off the walls of the White House cabinet room as if it was fired from one of VIRGINIA's cannons. All eyes were now fixed on the Elizabeth River.

Outraged at the disaster, Secretary of War Stanton screamed that the rebel ironclad might next "destroy every vessel in the service-lay every city on the coast under contribution-take Fortress Monroe-come up the Potomac and disperse Congress, destroy the Capitol and public buildings-or go to New York and Boston and destroy those cities!" But Stanton's dire predictions were not to come true, if MONITOR's commanding officer, Captain John L. Worden, had anything to do with it.

When VIRGINIA steamed from Sewell's Point to finish MINNESOTA, MONITOR was there to greet her. For the next four hours, the two ships circled and fired at each other from ranges no greater than forty yards without either side delivering a knockout blow. American and international journalists alike paid enormous sums for private boatmen to take them near the action but to no avail as clouds of black smoke from both ironclads obscured the battleground. Only the opposing crews had any idea who was gaining any advantage at all, and by the day's end both were certain only of their own ship's weaknesses.

Despite being half the size of her Confederate competitor, MONITOR from the start was an equal match for VIRGINIA. Because of her extremely flat decks, which were just inches above the water line, her turret presented the only sure target to the rebel gunners. And even if they scored a direct hit on the turret, which the Confederates did an estimated twenty-two times, the 120-ton mechanism was protected by a belt of eight-inch armor plating which measured twenty feet in diameter and nine feet high. Even though it was hard to stop once it began to revolve and harder for the guns crews to see the enemy from a small peephole, Ericsson's novel turret marked another advance in world naval technology. Everything went fine for the Federal ironclad until a shot from VIRGINIA smashed into MONITOR's pilot house, where Worden stood directing his ship. Blinded by metal splinters from the explosion, he was replaced by his executive officer Lieutenant Dana Greene.

Several times during the ensuing battle, both ships tried to ram the other, and it has been said that as both ships were so preoccupied with the other, the opposing pilots warned one another to avoid nearby shoal water. Nearing exhaustion and running low in ammunition, both ships finally pulled away without anyone able to discern properly who withdrew first. Journalists called it a draw as both sides declared victory. However, in a strategic sense, MONITOR had won since she was able to prevent VIRGINIA from doing any further damage. On the other hand, VIRGINIA was able to keep a large Federal navy force from sailing up the Elizabeth and recapturing Norfolk, Portsmouth, and the Gosport shipyard for two critical months while Porter and his shipwrights continued with other projects. During this period, tons of critical naval stores were shipped south and west to other rebel shipyards. In 1991, the famous battle was finally commemorated with the opening of the MONITOR-MERRIMAC Memorial Bridge-Tunnel which passes near the battle area from Suffolk to Newport News. As a footnote, the bridge-tunnel commission left the "K" off MERRIMAC(K) thus reopening the unfortunate debate about the correct spelling of her name, with local accounts favoring MERRIMAC.

To a large extent the Civil War, like any war, was decided by a contest of numbers. After VIRGINIA returned to dry dock for further repairs and improvements, the strangle hold of the Federal blockade only tightened and intensified by the day. Neither the Confederate political leadership in Richmond nor the genius of John L. Porter could hold off Lincoln's orders to wrench Gosport from the Confederacy. By May 10, 1862, orders were received from Richmond to abandon Norfolk, Portsmouth, and Gosport, and if possible, sail VIRGINIA up the James for the defense of Richmond. As Gosport was being burned a second time in two years, it was learned that the ironclad carried too much draft, nearly twenty-two feet, for the shallows of the James

River. Against the sentiment of many locals, VIRGINIA was subsequently scuttled on Craney Island in the early hours of May 11. Her magazines were fired, and as the crew looked on, she exploded.

Despite many false leads and the idealistic zeal of treasure hunters and archaeologists to find the wreck of VIRGINIA, nothing remains at the site. Just after the war, her machinery was salvaged and sold for scrap while whatever armor plating that could be saved was stacked along the Gosport fence for resale. The remaining hulk of VIRGINIA was salvaged in 1876 and brought back to Norfolk Naval Shipyard for scrap. MONITOR was lost that year off Cape Hatteras in a New Year's Eve storm and continues to be a Federally protected marine preserve. Her artifacts are on display at the Mariners' Museum in Newport News, Virginia.

As President Lincoln looked on from Fort Monroe, Federal troops under Major General James E. Wool made their unopposed amphibious landing at Ocean View on May 10, 1862, and recaptured Norfolk. Meanwhile Admiral L. M. Goldsborough's naval forces, this time with President Lincoln as a guest, sailed up the Elizabeth River to show the flag along the waterfront and retake Gosport, which was once again a smoldering ruin. However the Federals were pleased to find that Dry Dock I had again been saved with an extensive collection of pre-Civil War buildings. In addition to MONITOR, the former blockading fleet consisting of USS STEVENS, SUSQUEHANA, DAKOTA, SEMINOLE, SAN JACINTO and MOUNT VERNON anchored here before steaming up the James to bombard Confederate batteries along the bluffs before Richmond. Because of strict reconstruction ordinances, it would take nearly five years to bring the Norfolk Navy Yard, as Gosport was renamed after the Civil War, and the local maritime community back into full activity.

Both shipyard tradesmen and key personnel like John L. Porter, who worked for the Confederacy, were unable to find employment locally. Vital watermen like the Virginia pilots who had sided with the South were also legally excluded from practicing their trade after the war. However, after a long series of accidents including collisions and groundings, they were invited back to their old jobs by 1870. This time they conned commercial trade and United States Navy ships to and from Norfolk and Portsmouth as the Virginia Pilots Association whose headquarters was at the waterfront end of Freemason Street in Norfolk. One of the principal activities of the pilots and their navy counterparts during this period was removing wrecks and obstructions from local waterways, including the remnants of CSS VIRGINIA.

CHAPTER SEVENTEEN

Russian Bluebloods
and the Columbus Exposition

During the 1870s, naval activity in Hampton Roads picked up dramatically with the construction of the steam bark USS ALLIANCE and the eight-gun steamer USS GALENA at the Norfolk Navy Yard. All of GALENA's internal machinery and armament were also turned out in the yard's new foundry and machine shops, which marked a new era of marine industrialization for the region. Within the decade, a location for a second, larger dry dock was already designated. However one of the most exciting and colorful social events of the era came deep in the cold winter of 1877.

While staying in the Atlantic Hotel to pay a social call on the famous Russian opera director Max Strakosch, who was in Norfolk to sign local talent Adelaide Neilson for his next New York performance of *Romeo and Juliet*, Baron Shiskin, Russian Ambassador to the United States, wired his office in Washington that Norfolk and Portsmouth, including the Norfolk Naval Shipyard should be included on the Royal Russian tour. The Romanovs were represented by Czar Alexander II's son, Grand Duke Alexis, and brother, Grand Duke Constantine. Assigned to be the royal representative of the Russian Imperial Navy, Grand Duke Alexis was happy to accept an invitation to see the Elizabeth River harbor and its naval facilities, including the recently revitalized shipyard.

Fortunately, the visit, and in particular, the receptions,

given the Russian official party were preserved by local journalist H. W. "Scratch" Burton who wrote:

> *The Norfolk German Club, composed of our best young ladies and gentlemen, gave a complimentary German to Grand Duke Alexis, who honored the invitation by his presence accompanied by the following officers from the flagship SWETLANA: Rear Admiral Boutakoff, Prince Obolinski, Prince Nicholas Stcherbatov, Baron Shilling and others.*

On the evening of February 8, the United States Navy sponsored a dance that became one of the social events of that decade. Burton witnessed the event.

> *The dancing hall was adorned with the flags of all nations—both sides and the ceiling being covered— and bunting of various national colors. The ends of the hall were decorated respectively with flags bearing the Russian and American coat of arms, while the music and reception stage pyramids were formed of muskets, the burnished steel of which glittered brightly in the gas-light. The walls in the rear of the stages were hung with swords and cutlasses, and each corner of the room was occupied by a beautiful Gatling gun.*
>
> *Newly rebuilt shipyard shop floors had been decorated for the grand entrance of the Russian guests, escorted by the shipyard commandant Commodore J. Blakeley Creighton and most of Norfolk and Portsmouth's society. Dancing began just after the firing of the yard's famous 1866-naval timepiece, the nine o'clock gun, and continued past 2 A.M. the following morning with bands from the USS HARTFORD and Fort Monroe taking turns playing over nineteen reels.*
>
> *Following a reciprocal occasion on the SWETLANA, the Russians toasted the American navy officers and told them how impressed they*

were at seeing "one of the birthplaces of the United States Navy and the growing home of the American Atlantic squadron at Norfolk."

Because of its new recognition as a maritime and naval center, the region was subsequently chosen as the host for an International Columbian Naval Rendezvous formed here to commence the 400th anniversary of Columbus's voyage to America. Because of its magnitude and the subsequent goodwill that would follow, the event set the stage for the Hampton Roads rendezvous of the Great White Fleet in 1907.

According to Colonel William H. Stewart, a leader in the Columbus celebration, "On the 25th of April, 1890, Congress authorized the president to extend invitations to foreign nations to send ships of war to join those at the Norfolk Navy Yard in rendezvous at Hampton Roads and proceed thence to the review at New York.

"Pursuant to this, the 26th of April, 1893, was announced as the date fixed for the rendezvous. Another act of Congress provided for the construction in Spain of reproductions of two of the caravels of Columbus in order that they might be feature of the review and a third caravel, a duplicate of the largest vessel of Columbus, SANTA MARIA, was built by the Spanish government and sent across the Atlantic to participate in the celebration."

Boosted by a growing navy that would soon make its name in the Spanish-American War as both an Atlantic and Pacific Ocean power, the United States government was delighted to invite every navy in the world to send representative vessels to New York for a naval review to coincide with the opening of the Columbian Exposition in Chicago. A central location had to be found to form the great fleet which promoters heralded as the "greatest to ever be seen on earth."

Fortunately for the growing local tourist trade, Hampton Roads was chosen for the rendezvous location. Boasting about the great natural harbor, the first-class shipyard on the Elizabeth River and a host of smaller yards and marine facilities, supporters also used the region's rich history as a drawing card. Greater Hampton Roads claimed the sites of Jamestown and Yorktown, the epic Civil War battle of the ironclads CSS VIRGINIA and USS MONITOR. It could also boast on the construction site of the nation's first steel battleship and cruiser, USS TEXAS and RALEIGH at the Norfolk Navy yard, and the nation's first naval hospital.

The costs of putting on the show were another matter. Area leaders looked to Washington for help. Supported by local newspapers and practically every business from Old Point Comfort to Cape Henry, regional leaders organized a Hampton Roads Naval Rendezvous Association to lobby President Benjamin Harrison for financial support to entertain "immense throngs of visitors who will abide in our and the neighboring cities during the time allotted to the rendezvous in Hampton Roads." Secretary of Navy Benjamin F. Tracy, after examining the association's report and conducting a personal survey of the support facilities in Hampton Roads, sought an appropriation from Congress for $300,000 to support the venture.

Two factors then stalled the momentum. First, Harrison was a lame duck President. Furthermore, Congress was taking a Presidential election year lambasting for passing the nation's first billion dollar budget, which turned a surplus treasury into a deficit. Many Congressmen trying to hold their offices were also hiding a $90 million debt and most feared that further spending might cost them their jobs. The Naval Rendezvous Association replied that the invitations had already been sent. If Congress did not allocate the money, they argued, the United States would suffer international embarrassment. As the Norfolk *Virginian* reported, "The delay in Congress is causing some uneasiness in naval circles, and many officers are inclined to believe that the affair will prove a fizzle if speedy action is not taken."

At the last minute in March 1893, Congress appropriated enough money. By then seven nations had already sent their representatives across the Atlantic. Admiral Bancroft Gherardi, aboard his flagship PHILADELPHIA, was placed in command of the ships as they formed a line off Sewell's Point that would extend, bow-to-stern, for two miles.

Working closely with the Naval Rendezvous Association, Admiral Gherardi planned a series of parades, fairs, and fireworks displays designed to draw vast crowds to the area's hotels. Local merchants and watermen naturally rejoiced as sponsors began a successful, albeit last-minute, public relations drive across the nation. Fifty thousand posters depicting Hampton Roads with an inset portraying the battle of the Civil War ironclads USS MONITOR and CSS VIRGINIA were snapped up by various steamboat and railroad companies. As part of the public relations campaign, they were eager to display them in their landings and depots to draw tourists. A planned statue of Columbus at Fort Wool was also included on the poster. However it never went beyond the blueprint stage. Even a sham battle between the ironclads was planned.

According to the Norfolk *Virginian,* many people doubted the rendezvous would take place on schedule. Most of the American ships were still in the shipyard undergoing repair in late March and early April. Commanding Officers complained to shipyard commander Captain Edward E. Potter that they could not possibly get their ships to anchorage in time. Captain Potter answered, "We'll get you there on time even if my men have to sail with you!" And that they did. There was no tardiness on behalf of the twelve-ship American fleet.

Ironically a last minute diplomatic faux pas during an early arrival of the Royal Russian Navy flagship GENERAL ADMIRAL almost brought the celebration to a halt.

As the Russians passed Fort Monroe, they fired a twenty-one- gun salute honoring the United States flag. According to military protocol, the salute should have been immediately returned from the shore battery. Instead there was absolute silence as throngs along the beach in Hampton craned their necks in anticipation. However, the only sound from shore was an occasional murmur from the crowd that something terrible had gone wrong. Admiral Gherardi was equally puzzled as his sailors throughout the American fleet lined the rails for the salute.

Finally, the Russians sailed alongside USS PHILADELPHIA and fired a thirteen-gun salute in honor of the American admiral. Much to the embarrassment of everyone concerned, an uninformed and thus unprepared Fort Monroe battery finally returned the Russian twenty-one-gun salute nearly one hour later. Immediately, Admiral Gherardi sent a formal delegation to the Russian ship to apologize to the nation that was one of America's best friends during that period and to assure the Russian commander that rules of protocol would be strictly followed.

Despite some blustery weather that forced female visitors to anchor their skirts with lead shot sewn into their hems, the rendezvous began on April 17 with all the fanfare the celebration's backers had planned for. The harbor was described as "virtually alive with boats and ships of all descriptions," even though the number and size of the foreign vessels were considerably smaller than once hoped for because of the early schedule.

Among the most popular ships in the harbor were the colorful although awkward and cramped replicas of Columbus's trio, NINA, PINTA and SANTA MARIA, having been towed all the way by the Spanish Navy from Barcelona. For an entire week they and their modern consorts entertained thousands of residents and visitors alike.

With every hotel filled to capacity and local boatmen making five dollars per hour on every excursion to the fleet, the International Rendezvous was a financial success. It also focused national and international attention on Hampton Roads as the Navy's preeminent harbor.

Following a festive "Trades" parade through Norfolk, attended by more than thirty thousand people, and a fireworks display from the naval hospital, Admiral Gherardi led the fleet out of the Roads on April 24, and headed for New York. For Colonel William H. Stewart and others who participated throughout the rest of the celebration that was the four hundredth anniversary of Columbus's discovery of America, "Nothing surpassed the International Columbian Naval Rendezvous held in Hampton Roads for sheer beauty and majesty. It was judged by those who attended as the grandest of them all." Norfolk had earned international goodwill for the United States by hosting the Rendezvous and helped underscore her reputation as one of the world's great port cities.

CHAPTER EIGHTEEN

A Steel Cruiser Named Raleigh and a Battleship Called Texas

By the 1880s, the United States had fulfilled her manifest destiny across the continent and was building coaling stations into the Pacific. A collision with the Pacific and Asian territorial possessions of England, Germany, Japan, and Spain was seemingly unavoidable. A fight with Spain would come first as American naval forces found themselves engaged in the Spanish-American War after USS MAINE was blown up in Havana harbor on February 15, 1898. The opening shots of this war would help light the fuse for World War I and World War II and have profound effects on Portsmouth, Norfolk and the Navy.

To fuel the industrial might needed for global expansion, the coal fields of Virginia, West Virginia, and Tennessee were opened and an endless shipment of the black ore began to make its way to Norfolk by an ever-expanding rail. The readily abundant supply of coal and the growth of railroads was a major stimulus for the United States Navy to continue its expansion and interest in Hampton Roads. By 1900, Norfolk was the busiest coaling port in the world with terminals at Sewell's Point, Lambert's Point and Newport News served by the Norfolk and Western, Chesapeake and Ohio, and the Virginian Railroad companies. With the advent of the coal shipment business and the steady expansion at the Norfolk Naval Shipyard, both Portsmouth and Norfolk were not only fully recovered from the Civil War but destined to be the nation's preeminent Navy center.

As part of the shipyard's enlargement plan, a second dry dock was carved from the Elizabeth River shore. Just over 498-feet long, it was completed by 1889. Further down the yard's river front, an even more important naval technological event was about to take place-the construction of America's first steel battleship. And giving the harbor even more of a claim as the birthplace of United States Navy technology, the nation's first steel cruiser, USS RALEIGH was started next to TEXAS.

Equipped now with a railroad, steam power, and a telephone system, the shipyard was every inch the Navy's most advanced naval station and repair facility. The shift from a combination of wood and iron to steel in 1889 marked another radical turning point in marine architecture as tons of steel plates and girders began to roll into the yard.

Only a few yards from where the old frigate USS CHESAPEAKE was finished in 1801 and practically adjacent to Dry Dock I where USS MERRIMAC(K) in 1862 became America's first ironclad as CSS VIRGINIA during the Civil War, metal tradesmen began to out number woodworkers and carpenters. Instead of finding the sawing and bolting of wooden planking, visitors along the river now stood in awe while steel ribs were shaped, welded, and riveted together as if from a giant erector set.

With the cruiser RALEIGH preceding her by three months, America's first modern steel battleship, USS TEXAS, was launched into Elizabeth River on June 28, 1892, with a waterfront filled with an untold number of onlookers who no doubt knew they were witnessing history. Equipped with a battery of two 12-inch and six 6-inch rifles, the twin-screw, 6,315 ton-TEXAS was at least a decade ahead of the steam auxiliaries and older iron plated hulls commonly seen here. The size of her guns made her twice as lethal. Some skeptics criticized her lack of sail and rigging, and those still wedded to the wooden-hull days said that only a war could prove her "true metal in combat."

USS RALEIGH, also propelled by two screws and carrying a battery of eleven guns, was launched on March 31 amid similar fanfare and derision. She also had to prove herself in battle before the skeptics would accept her preeminence.

When war broke out against Spain in 1898, USS TEXAS

joined the Atlantic Squadron, part of which formed here in Hampton Roads and sailed for blockade duty off Santiago Harbor, Cuba. After American ground forces were unable to dislodge Spanish forces that had stubbornly fought against Colonel Theodore Roosevelt and his Rough Riders, the Spanish fleet made its move. A lookout in the American squadron yelled, "Smoke in the harbor. The fleet's coming out!"

On the American side there was a mad scramble for battle stations as bugles and pennants signaled the impending fight. On the Spanish side, four cruisers and two destroyers, led by the flagship INFANTE MARIA TERESA, steamed out in single file.

At 9:40 A.M., a pennant was hoisted aloft on the NEW YORK ordering the TEXAS and her sister ships to close and fight. Trying to outrun or ram the Americans, TERESA suddenly turned toward BROOKLYN which was barely 1,000 yards away. BROOKLYN pulled off to the right of the Spaniard to avoid collision. By this action, BROOKLYN was forced to continue starboard to gain her firing position on the enemy. Making the large right hand loop also placed her across the bow of TEXAS.

In one of American naval history's less memorable moments, Rear Admiral Winfield Scott Schley on the bridge of BROOKLYN barked to his navigator, "Damn the TEXAS, she must look out for herself!" Fortunately for TEXAS and her 310-man crew, commanding officer Captain John W. Phillip had the good sense to order both engines backed hard to prevent a collision. BROOKLYN and TEXAS were able to catch TERESA and finally disable her machinery, forcing her to run aground. A majority of the crew was killed and the ship destroyed when the magazine exploded. The American sailors stood and cheered as the Spanish pennant sank into the bay. When Captain Philip ordered lifeboats lowered from TEXAS to pick up the survivors, his order, "Don't cheer, boys, the poor devils are dying," made him a legend in his own time. Chief Engineer McAlphine, a Portsmouth native, also won praise at the battle as he managed TEXAS's engines far beyond their known capacity as the Americans traded shots with the enemy flagship REINA MERCEDES.

The next target for TEXAS and her sister ship OREGON was OQUENDO. This time the Spanish warship fought back fiercely with her 5.5-inch guns. As an enemy shell slammed into the bridge of TEXAS, Captain Phillip remembers, "pitching into the air with my coattails flying behind me as if I had been thrown by one of Theodore Roosevelt's broncos." Miraculously no one on TEXAS was killed, but Captain Phillip recalled that the "port cutter was blown into kindling, the woodwork of the superstructure was torn to bits and the ship took fire." Fire control parties soon had TEXAS back in action as shells from her guns and those of OREGON smashed OQUENDO into submission. After the surrender of COLON on July 3, Atlantic Squadron commander Rear Admiral William T. Sampson wired the Navy Department that, "The fleet under my command offers the nation, as a Fourth of July present, the whole of Cervera's fleet." Ironically, it was to the naval hospital in Portsmouth, the homeport of TEXAS, that many of the Spanish wounded were taken for treatment. Three of TERESA's enlisted crew died there and are buried in the hospital cemetery.

TEXAS returned to the United States several weeks later and steamed into her home port of Hampton Roads to a hero's welcome. For nearly three more years TEXAS patrolled the East Coast. In 1901, she returned to Norfolk Naval Shipyard for repairs, and in 1903 served as flagship for the Coast Squadron. Before her end, she passed several years as a station ship in Charleston, South Carolina; then in 1911 she returned to Virginia waters and was sent to the bottom of Chesapeake Bay as a target ship. Once a historic and gallant warship, she remains there to this day, rusting away in obscurity.

USS RALEIGH had equal fame in the Pacific campaign against the Spanish naval presence in the Philippines, winning accolades for her bombardment of the Spanish fortress Corregidor. A member of Admiral George Dewey's fleet who participated in the destruction of the Spanish fleet at Manila, RALEIGH provided vital support for the American amphibious assault at Subic Bay and destroyed the Spanish fort on Grande Island. Because of her open bridge and wooden masts, she earned the nickname, "The Armored Yacht."

Following the Spanish-American War, RALEIGH, like TEXAS, was given a hero's welcome home and honored by President McKinley. Following a distinguished career that took her to the Orient as well as to the coast of Africa and finally to U-boat patrol off the East coast of the United States, RALEIGH was sold for scrap in 1919.

CHAPTER NINETEEN

The Wright Brothers and a Moccasin

One historic incident that had both near-tragic overtones and comic relief was the nearly simultaneous events of the Wright brothers' epic first flight off the sand dunes of Kitty Hawk, North Carolina in 1903 and the almost simultaneous grounding of a locally-stationed submarine, USS MOCCASIN on the Outer Banks.

As the Wright brothers were almost finished with last-minute preparations to launch their experimental airplane off Kill Devil Hills, USS PEORIA began her tow of two submarines, MOCCASIN and ADDER, from Newport, Rhode Island to Annapolis, Maryland. Except for a storm that was growing off the coast of North Carolina and Virginia, the two incidents were separate. Just as PEORIA and her two customers were about to make the Virginia Capes, a northwest gale out of nowhere blew them about thirty miles off course in a southerly direction. Sometime during the pounding, the lifeline cable connecting the three ships broke, sending all three into disarray.

During the stormy night of December 2, the watch officer at the Norfolk Naval Shipyard put down his newspaper, which was full of stories about the impending flight of the Wrights, and took down the message that PEORIA, MOCCASIN and ADDER were in grave danger as they neared the Outer Banks, aptly called the Graveyard of the Atlantic. Within minutes the information was relayed to shipyard commander Rear Admiral Purnell Harrington, who quickly deployed the 185-foot long steel-hulled yacht YANKTIC toward the hapless PEORIA.

By daybreak ADDER was secured, but despite all efforts, MOCCASIN kept on her steady course to shore where she came to rest until January 4, 1904. Since most of the curious who had gathered around the Wright brothers were from United States Life Saving Station families, everyone dispersed to go to the submarine's rescue. As the epic first flight approached, newspapers reported a sparse crowd. Actual pictures show an almost empty sand dune as the Wright brothers took off. Meanwhile, down on the beach, hundreds had gathered to help and watch with something they had never seen-a submarine rescue!

The Wright brothers' flight was successful, of course, and the hapless MOCCASIN was finally refloated and brought to the Norfolk Naval Shipyard, joining ADDER for repairs. It is not recorded whether the Navy ever admitted that one of their submarines caused hundreds of people to miss the world's first propelled flight.

CHAPTER TWENTY

The Jamestown Exposition and a Great White Fleet

A NAVAL BASE IS BORN

More spectacles were on the horizon for Portsmouth and Norfolk and the Navy as the first decade of the twentieth century began with international focus again fixed on Hampton Roads.

Following in the wake of the 1893 Columbus Exposition, area leaders began the new century with a grandiose plan to mark the three hundredth anniversary of Jamestown with a world exposition. Without knowing it, they set in motion a series of events that would lead to the establishment of the largest naval installation in the world at Sewell's Point. The Norfolk Naval Base of today ironically enough would originate from the oldest Federal shipyard, a depression, a failed international exhibit, a Great White Fleet, and the beginning of World War I.

The creation of this vast naval complex goes back to the year 1903, when the vacant fields and marshlands of Sewell's Point were chosen as a commemoration site for the Jamestown celebration. No more spectacular and varied exhibition has ever in the continental United States been built. And even though it didn't last as long as the period it took to build, the exposition provided the foundation upon which the home of the Atlantic Fleet rests today.

On March 10, 1902, a charter was granted for the Jamestown Exposition Company with General Fitzhugh Lee, popular Spanish-American War hero and son of Confederate General Robert E. Lee, as president. The company was empowered to raise funds for a series of exhibits representing each state in the Union and most countries around the globe. A requirement of the charter was that one million dollars had to be subscribed by January 1, 1904— an unbelievable sum for that time period.

An open tract of 340 acres at Sewell's Point was selected and purchased in 1903. Everything from water power to electricity had to be brought in. Miles of bulkheads, piers and wharves had to be carved out of bogs. Telephones and lights had to be installed. Miles of sidewalks, promenades, and carriage ways were laid and built. All the amenities of a good size city were needed for the massive exhibit halls yet to come.

But despite the popularity of the project, leaders of the Jamestown Exhibition had difficulty raising the needed money. To shore up the effort, General Lee was joined by a board consisting of Nathaniel Beaman of Norfolk, first vice president; George F. Adams of Newport News, second vice president; and J.T. Wood of Portsmouth, third vice president.

In *Norfolk: Historic Southern Port,* historian Thomas Jefferson Wertenbaker described that last day of December 1903, with only a few hours left and more than a hundred thousand dollars still needed:

> *That evening a group of representative men gathered in the rooms of the Board of Trade, Norfolk, determining on heroic efforts to close the gap. Slowly but surely the remaining shares were subscribed, until at 11 o'clock only $5,400 was left. Ten minutes later the news arrived that a meeting at Newport News had taken $5,000. . . .*
>
> *'Who will subscribe the remaining $400?' it was asked. 'I will, on behalf of the Norfolk-Hampton Roads Company,'" said M.D. Lowenberg, director general of the exposition, and the great project was saved. . . .*

Sensing the importance and scope of the project, Congress authorized a million and a half dollars for Federal participation.

Construction crews continued work on a strip of road

paralleling the Elizabeth River to join Norfolk with the construction site, later named Hampton Boulevard. Even a trolley system connecting downtown Norfolk with the exhibition grounds was built. One of Norfolk's most beautiful neighborhoods, Ghent, was built to coincide with the exposition. Hotel accommodations for thousands of expected tourists were started in Norfolk, Portsmouth, and Hampton. Steamship and ferry lines were modified for the anticipated influx of exposition-goers.

It was indeed a monumental task, but work on the exposition grounds had progressed enough by April 26, 1907 to receive President Theodore Roosevelt and a host of other national and international dignitaries who followed behind the presidential yacht MAYFLOWER. After arriving at Discovery Landing at the foot of Raleigh Square, President Roosevelt led the official party up the marble stairs to the Court of Honor with its fountain flanked by a symmetrical pair of lagoons. The stately main auditorium beyond was opened for a reception and an official dinner. One eyewitness described it as "equal to anything experienced during the zenith of the classical Greek or Roman world. . . . As one strolls along the vast pavilions and colonnades, one can't help believe that he is nearing the center of western civilization!"

Always a consummate showman, President Roosevelt was now ready to play his best public relations card. As the waves of America's first twentieth century depression began to roll across the country, he announced that the United States Navy's entire fleet of sixteen battleships, manned by fourteen thousand sailors, would be sent to Hampton Roads that December for a cruise around the world! As these great "battlewagons" began to take on their fresh coats of white paint at the Norfolk Naval Shipyard, it was inevitable that they would be dubbed The Great White Fleet. No matter the color, Roosevelt's fleet meant badly needed dollars for Norfolk and Portsmouth.

On December 16, 1907, President Roosevelt watched the Great White Fleet steam past his yacht MAYFLOWER spewing their heavy plumes of black coal smoke and cinders over their pristine white decks. There was no doubt anymore that the United States was serving notice that she would compete aggressively to be the world's foremost naval power. No one at that time could have guessed what the Japanese response was to be. But looking back, the Great White Fleet's departure from here that December would have grave consequences for Hampton Roads, the nation, and the world in a December yet to come for Japan saw it as the beginning of America's challenge to her supremacy in the Pacific Ocean. The battleships that were led by Rear Admiral Robley "Fighting Bob" Evans that day included USS KEARSAGE, KENTUCKY, ILLINOIS, ALABAMA, MAINE, MISSOURI, OHIO, VIRGINIA, GEORGIA, NEW JERSEY, RHODE ISLAND, CONNECTICUT, LOUISIANA, VERMONT, KANSAS, and MINNESOTA.

Twenty ports of call on six continents awaited the sailors of the Great White Fleet in one of history's epic voyages in peace or war. True to form, President Roosevelt had added a touch of mystery and adventure to the voyage when he said to Admiral Evans before departure, "Now then, Admiral, one word before you go. Your cruise is a peaceful one, but you realize your responsibility if it should turn otherwise. As soon as you are at sea and feel the proper time, alert the crews that they are going around the world. Best of luck old fellow. Good-bye!"

The harbor would not see the Great White Fleet again until their triumphant return in 1909. As if closing forever a chapter of bygone days, each ship steamed up the Elizabeth to the shipyard for a fresh coat of battleship gray, which from that day has been the predominant color of United States Navy surface ships.

The lasting legacy of 1907 is the choice of Sewell's Point as the site for a naval base, a decision that can be traced directly back to the Jamestown Exposition directors. Within months after the departure of the Great White Fleet, the exposition crowds began to taper off. Some exhibitors went home while the administrators found it increasingly difficult to book new shows and programs to maintain local attendance. Within a year, the exposition ground had deteriorated drastically as the cost for upkeep continued to rise.

Within a decade, the exposition that had stirred the world's imagination was distinguishable only as a parched and peeling skeleton of its former self. The number of men working demolition crews often outnumbered those drawn to see the former glories. By 1917, only a miracle could have prevented the last vestige of the exposition from being razed. It took the intervention of President Woodrow Wilson and the beginning of World War I to save the remaining state pavilions that are now commonly referred to as Admiral's Row. The day after President Wilson declared war on Germany, Secretary of the Navy Josephus Daniels moved to purchase the entire site. On June 28, 1917, $2,800,000 was set aside for the original 367-acre Jamestown exposition grounds which measured 367 acres and 474 acres of adjacent land.

Thus the Hampton Roads Naval Operating Base was commissioned on Columbus Day, October 12, 1917. Within a month, the exposition grounds were turned topsy-turvy with a whirlwind of activity. Before the dust settled, the Naval Base expanded from 450 acres to more than 3,000, including a vast stretch of filled-in land. Fortunately, some of the more stately structures of the former exposition like Pennsylvania's replica of Independence Hall were adopted for other uses such as an officer's club. Now protected by historic landmark commissions, the remaining "state" homes are a fitting tribute to the builders of the Jamestown Exposition and a priceless collection of architectural treasures.

CHAPTER TWENTY-ONE

Hampton Roads Goes Over There

The establishment of the Norfolk Naval Base in 1917 marked an important shift in duty stations for the leaders of the Atlantic Fleet. The Norfolk Naval Shipyard in Portsmouth had since 1801 served as the area's principal government repair facility and operational headquarters site. With the Naval Base established at Sewell's Point, the "brass" of course moved across the Elizabeth River with their ships. However, this move did not break the close working relationship between shipyard and naval base. During World War I, that connection would be solidified when both institutions were called upon in an all-out effort to win the first battle of the Atlantic against the German and Axis navies. The economic landscape of Hampton Roads changed dramatically as well.

According to historian Thomas J. Wertenbaker, "In 1914 Norfolk's exports were $9,500,000 and imports $3,125,000; in 1926 exports had risen to $137,208,000 and imports to $16,868,000." The population of Hampton Roads had risen to a third of a million, buoyed by $220,000,000 in foreign trade and twenty million tons of waterborne trade. Indirectly, these jumps in population and commerce can be traced to the growth of the Atlantic Fleet and public and private support facilities along the Elizabeth River. At the beginning of World War I, before the United States had entered the conflict, Norfolk and the navy were actively involved in carrying out President Wilson's support program to the allies. A net effect was a rise in Hampton Roads exports from $9,500,000 in 1914 to more than $36,000,000 by

1916. The critical consequence of America's declaration of war on Germany and her allies on April 2, 1917, however, was on Norfolk's people.

Mass rallies were held throughout the city on behalf of navy recruitment and the manning of great warships like the battleship USS NEVADA. Along with the rallies and parades came the numbers which placed Norfolk first among national naval recruitment districts. By June 5, 1917, approximately ten thousand local men had registered under the draft act. Meanwhile on the waterfront, from Sewell's Point to Saint Helena, there was an endless parade of warships and freighters. The December 1, 1914 edition of the *Virginian-Pilot* best described the scene:

> *Great hulls from Norway, Sweden, and Denmark are uncamouflaged and beaten by the seas until they are the seas own gray. French barks and British merchantmen; ships from China and from Russia, from Argentina, and from the West Indies. The whole beautiful expanse of Hampton Roads is today populous with merchant craft that fly the flags of all the world. One can watch the harbor from dawn until dark, and the number and variety and fascination of the vessels seems endless. From either the Portsmouth or Norfolk side ships are seen taking on cargo and bunker at the great coal piers; still others are in the stream waiting their turn, while all about them ply the small, busy harbor craft, and an occasional big government dredge engaged in the work of making anchorages. In the distance, tramps and sailing vessels, barges and schooners show dim against the horizon.*

Second to coal colliers, wharves along the Elizabeth were next filled with troop transport ships. By the first of December 1918, the number of transports grew to 512 vessels totalling 3,246,000 tons. Over 288,000 troops left the local waterfronts for battle that year from the newly built United States Army Base terminal on Hampton Boulevard in Norfolk. Along with the doughboys a tremendous amount of munitions, uniforms, trucks, food, and other vital war supplies were shipped to Europe. To meet these shipment needs, rail lines and highways were added or radically altered in the direction of Sewell's Point and what is now the Norfolk International Terminal.

The development and enlargement of the Norfolk Naval Base itself began in the summer of 1917 with the establishment of a naval training camp. Noteworthy was the appearance of women sailors or "yeomanettes" at the base and across the river at the Norfolk Naval Shipyard. Augmenting the clerical staff at both facilities, yeomanettes made an invaluable contribution to the war effort by maintaining communication systems, payrolls, and supply records. Many volunteered to work the extra wards at the naval hospital in Portsmouth as well. By August of that year, barracks, mess halls, and storehouses for seven thousand recruits had been completed along with roads and three miles of railway. Construction along the Sewell's Point waterfront was extensive, including the 22,150-foot long bulkhead that cost over three million dollars. Massive backfill projects and thirty-five-foot deep-channel dredging proved to be tremendous challenges for the dredge barges and cranes, but the mud continued to fly day and night from 1917 through 1918. By the time they were finished, an additional three hundred acres had been added to the base.

To serve the needs of the growing fleet, two giant piers measuring 1,400 feet long and 125 feet wide were built into the Elizabeth River. Additionally, a submarine basin with a capacity for thirty-one vessels was built on the northwest side of the base, while on the north side a lagoon for seaplanes was constructed. Further to the east an airstrip for airplanes and dirigibles was built. Other building projects included hangars, two six-story warehouses, a cold-storage warehouse and ice plant, an aircraft storehouse, hospital wards, barracks, mess halls, machine shops, armories, officers' quarters, drill halls, laundries, garages and bakeries. All the facilities of a medium-sized city were built to support the Navy recruits, ships, and troops awaiting transport overseas.

Significant changes were also made at the Norfolk Naval Shipyard, which had already become the reluctant host of two German sea raiders. When KRONPRINZ WILHELM and PRINCE EITEL FREDERICK were captured and interned at the shipyard in 1915, the crew of about a thousand men began to build a miniature German village out of the yard's scrap metal and wood. Dubbed Eitel Wilhelm, the completed village with a German bakery, church and windmill drew hundreds of tourists. By the time the British passenger liner LUSITANIA had been sunk by a German submarine with the loss of 114 Americans and war declared by the United States, the two German ships had been scrapped, the village taken down, and the crews returned home.

The serious business of war preparations had already begun in earnest by 1916 with the Norfolk Naval Shipyard's employment figures running over eleven thousand employees. To spur the momentum forward, the facility became one of the first in the country to receive aid from the Navy bill of August 1916. According to official records, the "Norfolk plan," from which all other yards would follow, "embodied all the essential features of shipbuilding and repair, consisting of shipbuilding slips, dry docks, a structural shop, machine shop, foundry, a woodworking shop, storehouses, an administration building, a new power plant, and all the necessary auxiliary buildings." And just like the Norfolk Naval Base expansion, work soon began in earnest with the purchase of additional adjacent lands called the Schmoele tract.

Shipyard commander Rear Admiral Walter McLean was authorized to spend most of a $4.6 million budget by 1920 on modernization projects that included purchase of a 150-ton crane and a galvanizing shop. Next to building the new machine shop, which would become the nucleus of the yard during both World Wars I and II, the construction of what would become Dry Dock IV captured most attention.

Designed to handle the needs of the largest battleship afloat or on the drawing boards, Dry Dock IV took a sizeable chunk out of the Elizabeth River shore with its 1,011-foot length and 114-feet width. Before it was finished in 1919, 212 days ahead of schedule, it was designated by the Navy's Bureau of Yards and Docks as the greatest piece of mass concrete construction ever built in this country, based on the required removal of 625,000 cubic yards of earth and the pouring of 184,000 cubic yards of cement. Almost every yard statistic kept during World War I was broken during construction; it took over 850,000 board feet of solid oak timbers to form enough keel and bilge blocking to cover the dock floor. Yard engineers ran three lines of standard-gauge railway track around the outside lip of the dock, with two of the three tracks designed to carry the trucks of the fifty-ton service crane and a middle or third track built for yard locomotives and cars to clear the portals of the crane. The new Dry Dock IV was also equipped with three electrically driven Worthington centrifugal pumps, each with a capacity to move 14,400 cubic feet of water per minute. It could be filled in an astonishing two and a half hours.

At a total cost of five million dollars, Dry Dock IV set a national record when it received its first ship, the battleship USS WISCONSIN, just 26 1/2 months after the start of construction. Navy engineers who normally shy away from praise in their reports all agreed that Norfolk Naval Shipyard's newest dry dock was "an achievement unprecedented in the history of docks of comparable magnitude." Adjacent to number IV, Dry Docks VI and VII were underway as well. Completed in a record 18 months, the new smaller dry docks were opened in 1919 with the King and Queen of Belgium as guests of honor.

The Navy's Bureau of Yards and Docks also reported on the capabilities of the shipyard's new machine shop:

> *The enormous lifting capacities for the main aisles of 150 tons for a single crane and 300 tons for the two together are based on the greatest load expected to be handled, such as a modern turret for two 16-inch guns, completely assembled, with its armor and turning mechanism, weighing altogether about 290 tons; a 16-inch, 50-caliber gun weighing approximately 200 tons; a completely assembled boiler; a section of 14-inch side armor plate of 64 tons; or a completed basket mast for a battleship.*

Fueling the entire complex was a new power plant that at full capacity could produce 21,600 horsepower and generate 15,000 kilovolt-amperes. Needless to say, the lights never went out as Norfolk Naval Shipyard production shops went into full production on new ship construction projects that included twenty-one wooden, 110-foot-long submarine chasers, SC116 to 136, and the destroyers USS CRAVEN (DD-70), HULBERT (DD-342), NOA (DD-343) and WILLIAM B. PRESTON (DD-344).

By the time of the armistice ending World War I, a forest of United States Navy masts lined the Elizabeth River. Directly related to this boom in naval construction, major corporations like the American Chain Company, British-American Tobacco, E.I. Dupont de Nemours, Linde Air Products, Virginia Coal and Navigation, and Standard Oil joined the Norfolk Shipbuilding and Dry Dock Company in calling Norfolk home. With peace and a naval treaty limiting construction, however, the lights began to dim on the area's economy. It would be months after the celebrations and victory parades along Granby Street before the full effect of the war's end would hit the local economy, but there was no doubt at the naval base and shipyard that the growth period was over. Work on the forty-three-thousand-ton battleship USS NORTH CAROLINA (BB-52), already one-third complete, was brought to a halt.

Navy morale hit a low when NORTH CAROLINA was scrapped. All new physical improvements at both the yard and the naval base were canceled. Thousands of full-time and part-time employees at both installations and hundreds of others at private shipyards and navy-related business were laid off. As a direct result of the 1923 Washington Naval Limitation Treaty, employment at the Norfolk Naval Shipyard, for example, fell from the 11,000 mark in 1919 to 2,538 at the end of 1923. The United States Navy was by law forced to cancel all orders for new ships during the remainder of the 1920s and well into the next decade.

CHAPTER TWENTY-TWO

Airborne from a Covered Wagon

Even before World War I, many in Hampton Roads were looking skyward for new jobs and the Navy's future.

In fact, United States Naval aviation had already taken off in Hampton Roads on November 14, 1910 when stunt flyer Eugene Ely flew his airplane from a Norfolk Naval Shipyard-built platform on USS BIRMINGHAM in an experiment paid for by private money because Navy officials refused to support aviation advancement within their ranks. Even though Ely's flight nearly failed as he plunged from BIRMINGHAM and barely got his wheels above the waves, it was a start that would have the nation's military leaders at each other's throats and in and out of Norfolk as the argument raged about whether Naval Aviation was really the way of the future. Ironically it took an Army general named Billy Mitchell to convince key Navy officers and congressman that air power would be a primary factor in future naval tactics. Once again Hampton Roads became a testing ground for a historic change in naval technology.

With many skeptics and just a few supporters as witnesses, Mitchell oversaw the towing of captured German warships into the Chesapeake Bay in the summer of 1921 to serve as targets for American pilots. On the first run a navy seaplane sank a German submarine. Then a destroyer and the cruiser FRANKFURT were sent to the bottom. Finally, one of the strongest armored battleships in the former German fleet, or for that matter in the world, OSTFRIESLAND, was anchored and targeted. During the first try, Mitchell's airmen failed to sink the ship much to the audible relief of many of the navy old timers. But during an ensuing attack a formation of eight Martin-type bombers flying at twenty-five thousand feet dropped their payload of two-thousand pound bombs. Within twenty-five minutes, OSTFRIESLAND went bow-up and sank. Assistant Secretary of War Benedict Crowell would later claim that dozens of senior Navy officers wept openly as the great battleship was turned into a helpless hulk. Soon, however, as controversy continued to swirl around General Mitchell, the order went out to "build a ship capable of launching aeroplanes." The collier JUPITER looked like anything but the Navy's first aircraft carrier when it sailed into the Elizabeth at the end of World War I. A Navy coal carrier since her launch from Mare Island in 1912, she held the distinction of being the Navy's first electrically propelled ship. As she made her way from Mare Island to Norfolk, she became the first ship to transit the Panama Canal from west to east. On July 11, 1919 she was selected before the international limitations were formalized for conversion into an aircraft carrier. Navy officials, still very much in doubt about anything with wings, decided that starting a new ship from the keel up would be too expensive and that it would never be finished within the time limits of the treaty. Time and politics, however, were on JUPITER's side as she was taken over to the Norfolk Naval Shipyard for decommissioning on March 24, 1920. Her superstructure and decks were changed radically and inside arrangements modified for workshops and storage areas. No one expected a butterfly to emerge from the coal-dust-coated collier as hundreds of shipyard metal trades workers cut, soldered, and welded from the tops of her rigging down to her hold. Once the metamorphosis was complete, she looked as though a giant saw blade had cut away her rigging and replaced it with a giant erector set holding aloft a huge flat sheet of teak flight deck.

When JUPITER was recommissioned on March 20, 1922, she bore the name LANGLEY in honor off one of America's earliest pioneers in aviation, Samuel Pierpont Langley. From her 520-foot long and 65-foot wide "flying-off deck," rigged almost 63 feet aloft, crowds along the Elizabeth River witnessed the birth of the American aircraft era.

Appropriately for a pioneer ship, she earned the nickname Covered Wagon, a term which would stick during her career as a carrier and later when she went through another conversion as a seaplane tender. Although not very graceful at sea during her flank speed of fifteen knots, she was a formidable weapon of war nonetheless with her complement of fifty-five warplanes. A November 1922 edition of *Naval Institute Proceedings* described her rebuilt interior as "a combined floating aviation field hangar and repair plant for aeroplanes. The repair plant includes an armory, carpenter and wing repair shops, machine shop, blacksmith shop and foundry, metal shop, and torpedo repair shop besides photographic and aerological laboratories."

During the remainder of her shakedown period here, LANGLEY continued to make history. On October 17, 1922, Lieutenant Virgil C. Griffin piloted the first plane launched from her deck. On that day, as Griffin's plane lifted aloft, the era of American navy aviation began. For a brief time, planes leaving the LANGLEY were forced to land on a nearby beach or pasture, but barely a week after Griffin's take off, LANGLEY was the scene of the first full carrier launch and landing sequence as Lieutenant Commander Godfrey Chevalier wrote another chapter of naval history here. That same month, Commander Paul Whiting "took a leap" into the annals of Naval Air history as the plane he piloted became the first to be catapulted from the deck of LANGLEY.

Just before World War II began, LANGLEY received an order to deploy to the Pacific. After contributing significantly to the campaign against the Japanese, she was sunk in action south of Java on February 27, 1942. Her legacy of course will remain as the Navy's pioneer flat top.

Long before the bombs of Japanese warplanes brought the United States into World War II, the winds of war began to stir the harbor into action with the 1925 announcement of a battleship modernization plan. Calling for six of the fleet's oldest battleships to be brought to the Norfolk Naval Shipyard for new bridges, recalibration of weapons, and significant internal changes to spaces and propulsion systems. Battleships USS TEXAS, NEW YORK, NEVADA, ARIZONA, MISSISSIPPI and IDAHO steamed into port, bringing a shot in the arm to what had become after the war, a faltering waterfront economy. Even though the full effect of the Battleship Modernization Program did not completely shield Portsmouth and Norfolk from the devastation of national economic depression, it did lessen to some degree the severe apprehension of vast government layoffs that gripped the region.

Once again it took a Roosevelt to bring recovery. President Franklin Delano Roosevelt's July 1933 National Industrial Recovery Act contained a large plank for new naval construction. Once again funds began to flow into the Norfolk Naval Base and Norfolk Naval Shipyard for new buildings and equipment. Employment figures began to rise slowly at first from their low point of just 2,538 at the shipyard.

CHAPTER TWENTY-THREE

They Came from Shangri-La

As news hit Washington that the German war machine was rolling over western Europe, Navy officials began laying the groundwork for a new fleet to strengthen the overstretched and outgunned Atlantic Squadron that had only recently been formed. Even with the squadron's peak strength reaching four battleships, seventeen destroyers, eight cruisers, and a supply ship by 1939, it was impossible to properly escort American or allied merchant ships along the East coast or to adequately defend the Atlantic coastline from enemy attack.

Nonetheless, orders came down from Washington in 1939 that Norfolk would be the center of the operation to protect American waters from Newfoundland to the Caribbean. Setting the stage for what would grow in years to come to be the most powerful naval force in the world, the entire United States fleet visited Hampton Roads on its way to a review for the opening of the New York World's Fair. Out of the 140 vessels representing every maritime nation in the world, maintenance of 56 United States warships would be the responsibility of the naval base and shipyard. Within a year, both facilities' capacities were stretched further as the fleet grew to a total of 125 ships. During the war, that number grew to 708 ships.

The squadron was renamed the Atlantic Patrol Force with Rear Admiral Earnest J. King appointed as commanding officer. Ceremonies for his new position took place aboard the new battleship USS TEXAS. Soon after, Rear Admiral Randall Jacobs took command of the newly formed Base Force aboard the battleship USS WYOMING on January 2, 1941. Within a month, the Atlantic Patrol Force was designated an independent fleet, and when Admiral King was piped aboard, it was officially designated Atlantic Fleet with Norfolk as the headquarters. Now it was only a matter of time before local sailors would be on the front lines of another war.

In July 1940 naval base officials and yard management prepared for the arrival of battle-damaged allied warships. During his trip down the Elizabeth River on the yacht POTOMAC, Roosevelt told Fifth Naval District Commandant Rear Admiral J.K. Taussig, "For me this is a homecoming. As assistant secretary, I used to tell them in case of trouble, get Norfolk ready!"

However, many were not prepared for the beaten and battered hulks that began to creep into the harbor, mostly at night, to avoid German intelligence. If anyone doubted there was a war in the Atlantic, a May 1941 communique from Rear Admiral Taussig to Virginia pilot president Captain M.B. Edmonds announcing the arrival of the heavily damaged Royal Navy aircraft carrier HMS ILLUSTRIOUS dispelled any doubt.

Dear Captain Edmonds:

A damaged British man-of-war will arrive off Buoy 2-C-B at 8 Monday May 12, 1941. She is a very large ship and is to proceed direct to the Norfolk Navy Yard under cover of darkness. Caution, her lights will be used only when warranted. We hope to get her down the river and into the Yard without her character being detected.Will you please have one of your best pilots ready to board this ship at Buoy 2-C-B. A Navy Yard pilot will identify himself with the proper signals and also board the ship at the Cape.

Very truly yours,
J.K. Taussig
Rear Admiral USN

Virginia pilot Captain A.J. Bush was sent to meet ILLUSTRIOUS at the designated rendezvous, in a trip he and his fellow pilots would all too often take to meet damaged allied ships. During the battle of Malta, the 23,000-ton carrier had fought off a seven-hour attack from German dive bombers, sustaining six bomb hits and being set ablaze in the fore and aft sections. As the heroic ship swung between Norfolk and Portsmouth, downtown street lights illuminated her badly splintered wooden flight deck and twisted armor. She finally came to rest beneath the Norfolk Naval Shipyard's Hammerhead Crane at berth one.

The late Norfolk Naval Shipyard rigger Alfred "Red" Taylor described the condition of the British carrier when he and fellow workers went aboard:

We knew when we saw the ship that war wasn't too far off for us. She was in terrible shape. Holes from these bombs went right from the flight deck into the crew's mess areas. It was terrible down below. The first thing we were ordered to do was to get litters rigged and lowered to carry out the scores of dead sailors.

As a consequence, more British warships followed in ILLUSTRIOUS's listing wake to Norfolk including the battleship HMS ROYAL SOVEREIGN, the carriers HMS FORMIDABLE and INDOMITABLE, the cruiser HMS DAYTONIAN, and the escort carrier HMS ARCHER. Even though their presence at the Norfolk Naval Shipyard was considered classified, British sailors participated in a variety of cultural events during their stay, including little theater plays and Norfolk Symphony concerts. A public rugby exhibition was even given by the crews of HMS ILLUSTRIOUS and FORMIDABLE. German intelligence had apparently not developed a reliable network in the area as their national radio reported that neither ILLUSTRIOUS nor FORMIDABLE ever made it here, but were instead sunk at sea. Other allied ships made Norfolk their temporary home during the first years of the war, including the Dutch warship HNMS CLEASJE and the Soviet Navy's icebreaker KRASSIN.

By December 1941, Roosevelt's Arsenal of Democracy and

Lend-Lease programs were sending a flood of war materials and equipment to Great Britain from Portsmouth and Norfolk's wharves.

Suddenly during the early afternoon of December 7, 1941, all of Hampton Roads area was thrown into bewilderment and despair when news arrived that the Japanese Imperial Navy had launched an air attack against Pearl Harbor. Many remember those first moments of the war filled with great anguish and frustration because there was no way any of the dozens of Navy warships berthed at Norfolk or the shipyard could react. Even though armed guards patrolled outside the main gates of the naval base and shipyard, it was not until a declaration of war on December 8, 1941 that air raid warning sirens were sounded and anti-aircraft units were placed on the roofs of government buildings. The attack on Pearl Harbor was a national nightmare, but what was taking place in and around the waters of the Fifth Naval District was also horrible. To prevent a panic spreading throughout the area, the full dimension of German U-boat success off Virginia waters was kept secret for the most part.

Called operation "Drum Beat" by the German naval command, five enemy submarines prowled most of America's eastern seaboard during 1942 sinking allied and American merchant ships at will. America's concentration was on the Pacific at this time, and a coordinated effort to combat the German U-boat menace would not be launched until the later part of 1942. In the beginning, with just a few Coast Guard cutters and several destroyers to protect shipping in the Fifth Naval District, the Germans literally had an open season in area waters. Nearing the end of the war, the Fifth Naval District Public Information Office released the following assessment of U-boat activity:

> *At least 843 merchant seamen and naval gun crewmen of merchant ships gave their lives in action against the enemy on waters of the Fifth Naval District to keep supplies moving for the United States.*
>
> *Seventy-nine merchant vessels were ripped by Axis torpedoes, shells or mines, and 66 sank off Maryland, Virginia, and the part of North Carolina spanning Cape Hatteras, Cape Lookout, and Onslow Bay.*

*In these waters, which extend seaward half way to
Bermuda, the tonnage of the ships totalled 425,850.
Most of them went down off Hatteras and Lookout,
an area that bids highest in lives lost and tonnage
sunk for the title "Torpedo Junction."*

*But the U-boats also struck close to the Virginia
Capes, firing torpedoes or sowing mines that reaped
a harvest. Crowds at Virginia Beach once gazed at
a drama of sinkings staged only six miles away.*

Before long, some of the Norfolk Naval Base's supply
buildings were turned into makeshift morgues for some of the
843 allied merchant sailors killed off shore. The Portsmouth Naval
Hospitals and Norfolk naval clinics were filled with wounded.
Even though seventy-nine ships were lost, the flood of war
supplies for Great Britain continued.

The beginning of anti-submarine warfare against the German
marauders must have amused the enemy at first when many local
yachtsmen were asked to serve in a picket fleet to patrol local
waters. Virginia pilots also added their considerable talents to
this off-shore reconnaissance effort by taking commissions in the
Navy as they had done in World War I and before.

There was considerable work ahead for local Navy officials
to coordinate their anti-submarine efforts with those of nearby
army installations. But order finally settled over the chaos of the
first year of war, and by the end of 1942, Norfolk became a center
of anti-submarine activity that stretched from far out to sea with
Navy patrol and combat aircraft and destroyers to communications
centers at Cape Henry and across the Chesapeake Bay at Cape
Charles. Once the swept channel (a transit channel patrolled daily
for enemy activity including mining or other U-boat activity),
submarine nets and adjacent minefields were in place, the harbor
and nearby Virginia waters were made safe from further U-boat
attacks.

With squadrons of blimps droning overhead and hundreds
of patrol planes flying regular missions from Sewell's Point, plans
were drawn for what would become the Norfolk Naval Air Station.
Located at the Norfolk Naval Base, it is now one of the largest
and busiest military air stations in the world.

During this time and in spite of the German U-boat menace, one of the grandest naval war expeditions in history was planned in the Ocean View section of Norfolk at the Nansemond Hotel. In 1943 what became known as Operation Torch put to sea with hundreds of ships and thousands of American soldiers who successfully made it across the Atlantic to storm the beaches of North Africa and cut off valuable German oil supplies. War planners soon realized that the majority of the war's campaigns would begin with amphibious operations, so the Navy was given a directive to begin amphibious training at once while the shipyard and the Norfolk Naval Base began building and receiving a new class of warships, LSTs and LSDs. Navy officials chose the ferry landings at Little Creek along Norfolk's Chesapeake Bay shoreline to begin building what would become known as the Naval Amphibious Base, Little Creek. Today the enlarged facility shares the municipal borders of both Norfolk and Virginia Beach.

As the Atlantic Fleet began to grow with over one-third of the United States Navy homeported at Norfolk, thousands of sailors, marines, and airmen came to town, including hundreds of single women in the navy and in the civilian sector. For a time, city officials were barely able to handle the sudden influx. Apartment complexes and housing projects seemed to pop up overnight. As in World War I, World War II strained every civic service the city offered. New schools were built and others enlarged to accommodate military and civil service families that came to work at the base. The sidewalks of Granby Street and other major thoroughfares were jammed with sailors. One memory of that scene described it as walking in a "sea of white, starched uniforms-the air heavy with after shave lotion."

A whole new ferry system had to be routed to move the sailors and civilian workers between the numerous naval installations with satellite parking for the ferries spread out as far as the Craney Island Fuel Depot across the Elizabeth River.

The city's riverfront once again changed radically with the addition of a Navy submarine and destroyer complex southeast of the base along Hampton Boulevard and the addition of a training, storage, and repair facility at Saint Helena across the Elizabeth River from the Norfolk Naval Shipyard. Fortunately, the Navy had abandoned Fort Norfolk in the 1920s as an ammunition depot and had developed a site further up the Elizabeth River from the shipyard called the Saint Julien's Creek Annex to assemble naval gun shells and store munitions.

Some say the city was "never more alive, night and day, than during the war years." Despite strict fuel and food rationing, both Portsmouth and Norfolk were fortunate not to suffer the kinds of deprivation that other coastal and inland cities did. Once again the "marital" link between Portsmouth, Norfolk and the Navy held in a major international crisis. The jump in new jobs and income directly related to serving the fleet and the number indirectly affected by the war is incalculable. Both the Norfolk Naval Base and the shipyard doubled in size. Large private shipbuilding and repair facilities like the Norfolk Shipbuilding and Drydock Company also made significant contributions to the war effort and helped build the local economy. The Norfolk Naval Shipyard's employment figure rose to an all-time high of 42,893 in February 1943 with a similar rise at the naval base. For the first time women augmented the work force and held their own not only in the avalanche of clerical work, but also on the shop floors of the Naval Air Station and the shipyard.

An American archetype evolved from this work force. While walking around the construction site of USS ALABAMA looking for subjects for war production posters, Norfolk Naval Shipyard illustrator Shirley Hogge found a local woman working as a riveter. His several drawings of her with her nickname "Rosie" in the titles were sent to Washington where they reappeared on posters across the country. Here one of the first of the legendary "Rosie the Riveters" was born.

The Naval Shipyard's war effort was significant and remains unrivaled by any other repair facility. During the five years and eight months the yard was geared up for war production, the repair facility is credited with repairing, altering and converting 6,850 naval vessels, totalling over twenty-seven million tons. According to the yard's history, "at the same time, 101 new ships and landing craft were built for the fleet and millions of dollars worth of manufactured products were turned out for the forces afloat and for other naval establishments." The yard's production in World

War II reached the staggering total of well over one billion dollars. Major changes to the yard waterfront included a new 1,100 foot dry dock, 689 new buildings, and increase of reservation size from 353 acres to 747 acres.

The growth of Navy and U.S. Marines facilities also crossed into neighboring Princess Anne County (Virginia Beach) with the creation of Oceana Naval Air Station and Dam Neck's training center.

The employment figures and output in services for both the base and the yard remained fairly consistent to the end of World War II and throughout the Cold War that followed. They represent hard evidence of how valuable Portsmouth and Norfolk had become as the unofficial "Capitol" of the United States Navy, a mantle of distinction that both have worn with pride ever since.

Certainly no city surpasses their war record as ships with names like TUCKER, DOWNES, BAGLEY, BLUE, HELM, ROWAN, STACK, MORRIS, WAINWRIGHT, WAHTAH, RAVEN, OSPREY, AUK, HERNDON, ALABAMA, SHUBRICK, KENTUCKY, REUBEN JAMES, SIMS, HOPPING, REEVES, FECHTELER, CHASE, BARBER, LANING, LOY, LOVELACE, SHANGRI-LA, LAKE CHAMPLAIN and TARAWA, rose from the shipyard buildingways in Portsmouth and were commissioned at the Norfolk Naval Base. In addition, the yard built 20 landing ship tanks of 3,776 tons each. No doubt the energy from this momentum that played such a significant role in winning World War II carried the area and the Navy together into an era of atomic weaponry and nuclear propulsion.

CHAPTER TWENTY-FOUR

Dual Hat City

Following the end of World War II Norfolk became not only the homeport and headquarters for the Atlantic Fleet, but also the headquarters for the Supreme Allied Command, Atlantic. Complete with a new Armed Forces Staff College, now part of the National Defense University, on Hampton Boulevard, the navy turned the World War I-vintage naval hospital compound off Hampton Boulevard into a new headquarters for not only the Atlantic Fleet and Supreme Allied Command, but also for the new command divisions or "type" commands for training, air, submarine and surface forces. More than 300 ships pulled in and out of the Elizabeth River on their new patrol assignments during the 1950s and 1960s against the growing menace of the Soviet Navy. With communist naval commitments along the coast of Africa and by 1961 in nearby Cuba, Hampton Roads' was not allowed time after World War II to return to a full peacetime operation tempo. As war broke out in Korea during the early 1950s, the Norfolk Naval Shipyard and the Naval Base went back to a wartime schedule as critical supplies, personnel, and materials were shipped out around the clock.

During the Korean War, Norfolk became home for the Navy "battlewagons" with the arrival of USS MISSOURI and then the USS NEW JERSEY. USS MISSISSIPPI and USS IOWA followed in their wake. While in Norfolk Naval Shipyard, the battleship USS WISCONSIN got a giant nose job as the bow of the unfinished USS KENTUCKY was removed and fixed to that of USS WISCONSIN in 1957. Two wooden-hull minesweepers, the last two ships to be built at the Norfolk Naval Shipyard, were launched in March 1953. Unfortunately, the weathered relic USS HARTFORD, flagship of Admiral David Farragut during the Civil War battle of Mobile Bay, was left unattended at Saint Helena and sunk. Following an official survey which led to her condemnation, she was moved to Craney Island and burned. There must have been plenty of solid timber in her, however, for it took several attempts to destroy her. Many lament today that HARTFORD was not restored and tied alongside the shipyard waterfront. But concentration, energy, and finances were focused elsewhere during those days of the Cold War. Fortunately a number of her artifacts, including her stern emblem and two sideboards, were preserved by the Portsmouth Naval Shipyard Museum, where they still may be seen.

The work tempo increased during the mid-1960s through the early 1970s as the Vietnam War intensified. During this time the yard became the preeminent aircraft carrier repair facility in the nation. Once again Norfolk Naval Base terminals were busy around the clock with the departure of ships, marines, and essential war materials.

Today, worldwide commitments that take Atlantic Fleet ships to the North and South Atlantic, Mediterranean Sea, Persian Gulf, Adriatic, and Indian Ocean have kept Portsmouth and Norfolk on the frontline of America's post-Cold War determination to secure the peace. In the recent war with Iraq, "Desert Shield, Desert Storm," the Atlantic Fleet were called upon once more for front line duty and they answered the call.

Together the Portsmouth and Norfolk communities and the Navy have lived as a family through hard times, lean times, and shared mutual embarrassment and tragedy. Thousands of residents held their breath as dozens of navy tugs tried to push and pull a grounded USS MISSOURI off the mud banks of Hampton from January 17 to February 1 in 1950. From the days following the Vietnam War when national politics had turned negative about the navy to the shocking news that American marines had been killed in their barracks while on a peacekeeping mission in Beirut, Lebanon, Norfolk and the Navy bore together their mutual grief. This same caring attitude followed the battleship IOWA turret explosion. Local civilians and military families alike reached out to the ship and helped the command regain its confidence and strength. No other community in the world now has such a record and relationship with her Navy as Portsmouth and Norfolk, Virginia.

CHAPTER TWENTY-FIVE

A Marriage Built to Last

Today, the Norfolk Naval Base is the center of the largest naval complex in the world. Her size does not lessen her quality nor her determination to serve the Atlantic Fleet first and foremost with the highest quality service possible.

Navy and civic leaders alike emphasize that it is local people, both in uniform and civilian clothes, who truly guarantee that this quality will continue. A prepared and battle-ready fleet is Hampton Roads's daily focus and product. As home of the newest nuclear-powered aircraft carriers, the Aegis-class guided-missile destroyers and cruisers, the most sophisticated amphibious ships, advanced submarines and airplanes in the world, the traditional partnership between the Navy and Portsmouth and Norfolk continues full steam into the future.

Following in the tradition of the first frigates, CHESAPEAKE, CONSTELLATION and CONSTITUTION, powerful new warships that carry names like HARRY S. TRUMAN, THEODORE ROOSEVELT, GEORGE WASHINGTON, JEFFERSON CITY, WASP, and ARLEIGH BURKE call Hampton Roads their home.

A sturdy foundation and confidence in one another can only come from a tradition well deserved and respected—one for the other in the cause of insuring America's democracy and freedom of the seas for the twenty-first century. It is indeed a marriage that was built, like our Navy's ships, to last.

APPENDIX A

FORMER SHIPYARD COMMANDERS NORFOLK NAVAL SHIPYARD

NAME	FROM / TO	HULLS HONORING
Captain Richard Dale	1794–July 1794	SLOOP-OF-WAR DD-4, DD-290, DD-358, DLG-19
William Pennock	July 1794–30 April 1798	
Captain Thomas Williams	30 April 1798–16 July 1799	
Captain Samuel Barron	16 July 1799–August 1799	
William Pennock	August 1799–26 April 1802	
Daniel Bedinger	26 April 1802–10 February 1808	
Theodorick Armistead	10 February 1808–7 July 1810	
Captain Samuel Barron	7 July 1810–10 November 1810	
Lieutenant Robert Henley	10 November 1810–1 May 1811	DD-39, DD-391
Captain Samuel Evans	1 May 1811–10 August 1812	
Captain John Cassin	10 August 1812–1 June 1821	
Captain Lewis Warrington	1 June 1821–1 December 1824	
Captain James Renshaw	1 December 1824–25 May 1825	
Captain James Barron	25 May 1825–26 May 1831	
Captain Lewis Warrington	26 May 1831–7 October 1840	DD-30, DD-383, DD-843
Captain William B. Shubrick	7 October 1840–1 October 1843	STEAMER TB-31, DD-268, DD-639
Captain Jesse Wilkinson	1 October 1843–1 October 1846	
Captain Charles W. Skinner	1 October 1846–1 June 1847	
Captain Lawrence Kearney	1 June 1847–19 January 1848	DD-432
Captain John D. Sloat	19 January 1848–17 February 1851	DD-316, DE-245
Captain Silas H. Stringham	17 February 1851–1 April 1852	TB-19, DD-83
Captain Samuel L. Breese	1 April 1852–10 May 1855	
Captain Issac McKeever	10 May 1855–6 May 1856	
Captain Thomas A. Dornin	6 May 1856–30 April 1859	
Captain Charles H. Bell	30 April 1859–1 August 1860	
Captain Charles S. McCauley	1 August 1860–20 April 1861	
*Captain Robert B. Pegram	21 April 1861–22 April 1861	
**Captain French Forres	22 April 1861–1 July 1861	
***Captain French Forrest	1 July 1861–15 May 1862	CSS *St Tug*

127

NAME	FROM / TO	HULLS HONORING
****Captain Sidney S. Lee	15 May 1862–20 May 1862	
Como. John W. Livingston	20 May 1862–16 November 1864	
Captain John M. Berrien	16 November 1864–31 October 1865	
Como. Robert B. Hitchcock	31 October 1865–7 August 1866	
R.Adm. Stephen C. Rowan	7 August 1866–15 August 1867	TB-8, DD-64, DD-405, DD-782
Como Augustus H. Kilty	15 August 1867–1 October 1870	DD-137
R. Adm. Charles H. Davis	1 October 1870–1 July 1873	TB-12, DD-65, DD-395, DD-937
Como. Thomas H. Stevens	1 July 1873–1 July 1876	DD-86, DD-479
Como. J. Blakeley Creighton	1 July 1876–1 July 1879	
Como. Aaron K. Hughes	1 July 1879–3 July 1882	
Como. William K. Mayo	3 July 1882–10 April 1885	
Como. William T. Truxton	10 April 1885–11 March 1886	
Como. George Brown	11 March 1886–14 January 1890	
Como. Aaron W. Weaver	14 January 1890–16 January 1893	
Captain Edward E. Potter	16 January 1893–29 July 1893	
R.Adm. George Brown	29 July 1893–1 June 1897	
R.Adm. Norman H. Farquhar	1 June 1897–5 October 1899	DD-304, DE-139
R.Adm. Albert S. Barker	5 October 1899–16 July 1900	DD-213
R.Adm. Charles S. Cotton	16 July 1900–1 April 1903	
R.Adm Purnell F. Harrington	1 April 1903–7 July 1906	
R.Adm. Robert H. Berry	7 July 1906–26 December 1907	
R.Adm. Edward D. Taussig	26 December 1907–20 November 1909	DD-746
R.Adm.William A. Marshall	20 November 1909–1 November 1911	
R.Adm. Robert M. Doyle	1 November 1911–1 December 1913	
R.Adm. Nathaniel R. Usher	1 December 1913–25 Sept 1914	
#Como. Louis R. deSteiguer	25 Sept 1914–4 January 1915	
R.Adm. Frank E. Beatty	4 January 1915–25 November 1915	DD-640, DD-756
R.Adm. Walter McLean	25 November 1915–4 February 1918	
R.Adm. A. F. Fechteler	5 February 1918–10 April 1919	DE-157, DD-870
#Captain B. F. Hutchison	10 April 1919–15 November 1919	
R.Adm. Guy H. Burrage	15 November 1919–1 July 1921	
R.Adm. Philip Andrews	1 July 1921–6 June 1923	
R.Adm. Henry J. Ziegemeier	6 June 1923–10 January 1925	
#Captain Clarence S. Kempff	10 January 1925–18 May 1925	

NAME	FROM / TO	HULLS HONORING
#Captain William T. Tarrant	18 May 1925–16 November 1925	
R. Adm. William C. Cole	16 November 1925–2 July 1928	DE-641
R.Adm. Wat T. Cluverius	2 July 1928–31 May 1930	
R.Adm. Frank H. Brumby	31 May 1930–28 Sept 1932	
#Captain William N. Jeffers	28 Sept 1932–14 February 1933	DD-621
R. Adm. A. St. Clair Smith	14 February 1933–23 July 1935	
R.Adm. Charles S. Freeman	23 July 1935–15 October 1937	
#Captain L. P. Treadwell1	5 October 1937–22 November 1937	
R.Adm. Manley H. Simons	22 November 1937–17 June 1941	
#Captain L. P. Treadwell	17 June 1941–1 August 1941	
R.Adm. Felix X. Gygax	1 August 1941–19 October 1944	
R.Adm. Carl H. Jones	19 October 1944–1 December 1945	
Como. Lisle F. Small	1 December 1945–1 November 1946	
#Captain Noah W. Gokey	1 November 1946–19 March 1947	
R.Adm. Homer N. Wallin	18 February 1949–15 February 1951	
R.Adm. David H. Clark	15 February 1951–30 June 1953	
#Captain William H. Leahy	30 June 1953–11 August 1953	
R.Adm. Logan McKee	11 August 1953–13 Sept 1956	
R.Adm. G. A Holderness, Jr.	13 Sept 1956–30 June 1958	
R.Adm. William H. Leahy	30 June 1958–29 June 1960	
R.Adm. W.E. Howard, Jr.	29 June 1960–28 June 1963	
R.Adm. James M. Farrin	28 June 1963–30 June 1965	
R.Adm. James A. Brown	30 June 1965–27 June 1970	
R.Adm. Jamie Adair	27 June 1970–4 June 1972	
R.Adm. Randolph W. King	24 June 1972–22 June 1973	
R.Adm. Joe Williams, Jr.	22 June 1973–31 August 1974	
R.Adm. Elmer T. Westfall	31 August 1974–25 June 1977	
Captain A. Kurzenhauser	25 June 1977–26 July 1980	
Como. David P. Donohue	26 July 1980–29 April 1983	
Captain Michael R. Gluse	29 April 1983–12 June 1987	
Captain E. S. McGinley	12 June 1987–11 May 1990	
R.Adm. James L. Taylor	11 May 1990–12 August 1994	
Captain Willam R. Klemm	12 August 1994–8 August 1997	
Captain Timothy E. Scheib	8 August 1997–Present	

*Captain Robert Pegram-Virginia State Navy
**Captain French Forrest-Virginia State Navy
***Captain French Forrest-Confederate States Navy
****Captain Sydney Lee-Confederate States Navy
#Acting Commander

APPENDIX B

BUILT/CONVERTED SHIPS at the NORFOLK NAVAL SHIPYARD

CHESAPEAKE frigate, 36 guns, 1244 tons, keel laid December 10, 1798, launched December 2, 1799

FERRET cutter, 12 guns, length on deck 73', built 1806-1809 GUNBOATS 146 to 155—length approx. 50' built 1808-1810

DELAWARE ship, 74 guns, 2633 tons, keel laid August 1817, launched October 21, 1820

NEW YORK ship, 74 guns, 2633 tons, keel laid 1818, never completed, burned on the stocks by evacuating Federal forces

ST. LAWRENCE frigate, 44 guns, 1708 tons, keel laid 1826, launched March 25, 1847

NATCHEZ sloop, 20 guns, 691 tons, built 1827

JOHN ADAMS sloop, 20 guns, 700 tons, keel laid 1829, launched November 17, 1830

MACEDONIAN frigate, 36 guns, 1341 tons, keel laid 1832, launched 1836

PIONEER brig, 6 guns, 230 tons, built 1836

YORKTOWN sloop, 16 guns, 566 tons, keel laid 1838, launched June 17, 1839

GERM experimental horizontal paddle wheel, steam craft, built 1841

UNION steam schooner, 4 guns, 956 tons, keel laid 1841, launched May 12, 1842

TRUXTUN brig, 10 guns, 331 tons, keel laid 1842, launched April 16, 1842

SOUTHAMPTON storeship, 4 guns, 567 tons, keel laid 1842, launched 1845

PERRY brig, 10 guns, 280 tons, keel laid February 18, 1843, launched May 9, 1843

JAMESTOWN sloop, 20 guns, 1150 tons, keel laid 1843, launched September 16, 1844

POWHATAN steam bark, side-wheel, 9 guns, 2415 tons, keel laid August 6, 1847, launched February 14, 1850

CONSTELLATION corvette, 24 guns, 1278 tons, keel laid 1853, launched August 26, 1854

ROANOKE steam frigate, screw, 40 guns, 3400 tons, launched December 13, 1855

COLORADO steam frigate, screw, 40 guns, 3400 tons, keel laid May 1854, launched June 19, 1856

DACOTAH steam sloop, screw, 6 guns, 998 tons, keel laid 1858, launched March 23, 1859

RICHMOND steam sloop, screw, 14 guns, 2700 tons, keel laid 1858, launched January 26, 1860

POCAHONTAS steam sloop, screw, 5 guns, 694 tons, rebuilt and enlarged from 558 to 694 tons

VIRGINIA ironclad ram, steam screw, 10 guns, 3200 tons, constructed from steam frigate MERRIMACK

RICHMOND ironclad ram, steam screw, 4 guns, length 180', keel laid 1861, launched May 6, 1862

NANSEMOND gunboat, wood, steam screw, 2 guns, 80 tons, built 1862

HAMPTON gunboat, wood, steam screw, 2 guns, 80 tons, built 1862

NORFOLK gunboat, wood, steam screw, building 1862, burned on the stocks by evacuating Confederate forces

PORTSMOUTH gunboat, wood, steam screw, building 1862, burned on the stocks by evacuating Confederate forces

ESCAMBIA gunboat, wood, iron protected, 2 guns, construction begun, burned on the stocks by evacuating Confederate forces

ELIZABETH gunboat, wood, iron protected, 2 guns, construction begun, burned on the stocks by evacuating Confederate forces

YADKIN gunboat, wood, iron protected, 2 guns, construction begun, burned on the stocks by evacuating Confederate forces

GALENA steam sloop, screw, 8 guns, 1900 tons, built 1871-1879

ALLIANCE steam bark, wood, screw, 6 guns, 1375 tons, keel laid 1873, launched March 8, 1875 as the Huron

DAISY steam, ferry, wood, length 64' 6", built 1885

TEXAS battleship, twin screw, main battery—two 12" and six 6" rifles, 6315 tons, keel laid June 1, 1889, launched June 28, 1892

RALEIGH cruiser, twin screw, 11 guns, 3183 tons, keel laid December 15, 1889, launched March 31, 1892

AMPHITRITE Monitor, twin screw, double turrets, 4 guns, 3990 tons, rebuilt 1890-1894

SAMOSET harbor tug, steel, 225 tons, keel laid January 13, 1896, launched March 20, 1897

COURIER steam ferry, wood, length 56' 8", built 1897

NAVY YARD steam ferry, composite, length 80', built 1901

GALVESTON cruiser, twin screw, 10 guns, 3200 tons, construction completed February 15, 1905

INDIAN steam ferry, wood, length 60' 9", built 1906

PATUXENT ocean tug, steel, 755 tons, keel laid July 25, 1907, launched May 16, 1908

CHEMUNG ocean tug, steel, 575 tons, keel laid October 2, 1915, launched April 1, 1916 as the POCAHONTAS

SUBMARINE CHASER SSC-116 TO 136—21 vessels, wood, 110' long, triple screw, built 1917-1918

CRAVEN DD-70—destroyer, 1125 tons, keel laid November 20, 1917, launched June 29, 1918

HULBERT DD-342, destroyer, four funnels, 1215 tons, keel laid November 18, 1918, launched June 28, 1919

NOA DD-343, destroyer, four funnels, 1215 tons, keel laid November 18, 1918, launched June 28, 1919

WM. B. PRESTON DD-344, destroyer, four funnels, 1215 tons, keel laid November 18, 1918, launched August 9, 1919

LANGLEY CV-1, aircraft carrier, 12700 tons, electrically propelled, converted from JUPITER 1919-1922

NORTH CAROLINA BB-52, battleship, 43200 tons, keel laid January 12, 1920, construction suspended February 8, 1922 and scrapped in accordance with treaty limiting Naval Armaments

TEXAS BB-35, battleship, 27000 tons, modernized 1925-1926

NEW YORK BB-34, battleship, 27000 tons, modernized 1926-1927

NEVADA BB-36, battleship, 29000 tons, modernized 1927-1929

ARIZONA BB-39, battleship, 32600 tons, modernized 1929-1931

MISSISSIPPI BB-41, battleship, 33000 tons, modernized 1931-1933

IDAHO BB-42, battleship, 33400 tons, modernized 1931-1934

TUCKER DD-374, destroyer, 1500 tons, keel laid August 15, 1934, launched February 26, 1936

DOWNES DD-375, destroyer, 1500 tons, keel laid August 15, 1934, launched April 22, 1936

BAGLEY DD-386, destroyer, 1500 tons, keel laid July 31, 1935, launched September 3, 1936

BLUE DD–387, destroyer, 1500 tons, keel laid September 25, 1935, launched May 27, 1936

HELM DD–388, destroyer, 1500 tons, keel laid September 25, 1935, launched May 27, 1937

ROWAN DD–405, destroyer, 1500 tons, keel laid June 25, 1937, launched May 5, 1938

STACK DD–406, destroyer, 1500 tons, keel laid June 25, 1937, launched May 5, 1938

MORRIS DD–417, destroyer, 1570 tons, keel laid June 7, 1938, launched June 1, 1939

WAINWRIGHT DD–419, destroyer, 1570 tons, keel laid June 7, 1938, launched June 1, 1939

RAVEN AM–55, minesweeper, 756 tons, keel laid June 28, 1939, launched August 24, 1940

OSPREY AM–56, minesweeper, 744 tons, keel laid June 28, 1939, launched August 24, 1940

WAHTAHY TB–140, harbor tug (big), 237 tons, keel laid August 28, 1939, launched December 14, 1939

YF–257 covered lighter (self propelled), keel laid January 31, 1940, launched June 29, 1940

ALABAMA BB–60, battleship, 35000 tons, keel laid February 1, 1940, launched February 16, 1942

YF–287 covered lighter (self propelled), keel laid February 21, 1941, launched May 3, 1941

AUK—AM–57 minesweeper, 890 tons, keel laid April 15, 1941, launched August 26, 1941

YW–59 water barge (self propelled), keel laid July 26, 1941, launched August 29, 1941

HERNDON DD–638, destroyer, 1630 tons, keel laid August 26, 1941, launched February 5, 1942

SHUBRICK DD–639, destroyer, 1630 tons, keel laid February 17, 1942, launched April 18, 1942

KENTUCKY BB–66, battleship, 45000 tons, keel laid March 7, 1942, construction suspended April 17, 1946; scrapped 70 percent complete

LANDING CRAFT, MECHANIZED LCM, 50 vessels, 50' in length, program started May 20, 1942, completed August 21, 1942

LANDING SHIPS, TANK LST–333 TO 352, 20 vessels, 1625 tons, program started July 17, 1942, completed February 7, 1943

REUBEN JAMES DE-153, escort vessel, 1400 tons, keel laid September 7, 1942, launched February 6, 1943

SIMS DE-154, escort vessel, 1400 tons, keel laid September 7, 1942, launched February 6, 1943

YSD-38 seaplane wrecking derrick, keel laid November 10, 1942, launched January 16, 1943

HOPPING DE-155 escort vessel, 1400 tons, keel laid December 15, 1942, launched March 10, 1943

SHANGRI-LACV-38, aircraft carrier, 27100 tons, keel laid January 15, 1943, launched February 24, 1944

YSD-39 seaplane wrecking derrick, keel laid January 18, 1943, launched March 8, 1943

REEVES DE-156, escort vessel, 1400 tons, keel laid February 7, 1943, launched April 22, 1943

FECHTELER DE-157, escort vessel, 1400 tons, keel laid February 7, 1943, launched April 22, 1943

YSD-40 seaplane wrecking derrick, keel laid March 8, 1943, launched May 6, 1943

LAKE CHAMPLAIN CV-39, aircraft carrier, 27100 tons, keel laid March 15, 1943, launched November 2, 1944

CHASE DE-158, escort vessel, 1400 tons, keel laid March 16, 1943, launched April 24, 1943

YRD(H)-3 workshop, floating dry dock (hull), keel laid April 1, 1943, launched May 14, 1943

YRD(M)-3 workshop, floating dry dock (machinery), keel laid April 5, 1943, launched May 14, 1943

LANING DE-159, escort vessel, 1400 tons, keel laid April 23, 1943, launched July 4, 1943

LOY DE-160, escort vessel, 1400 tons, keel laid April 23, 1943, launched July 4, 1943

BARBER—DE-161 escort vessel, 1400 tons, keel laid April 27, 1943, launched May 20, 1943

YSD-41 seaplane wrecking derrick, keel laid May 7, 1943, launched June 16, 1943

LOVELACEDE-198, escort vessel, 1400 tons, keel laid May 22, 1943, launched July 4, 1943

ATHERTON—DE-169 escort vessel, 1240 tons, transferred to NNSY June 23, 1943 when 73% complete, completed September 17, 1943

BOOTH—DE–170 escort vessel, 1240 tons, transferred to NNSY June 26, 1943 when 57% completed; completed September 30, 1943

CARROLL—DE–171 escort vessel, 1240 tons, transferred to NNSY June 26, 1943, when 53% complete; completed November 8, 1943

THOMAS—DE–102 escort vessel, 1240 tons, transferred to NNSY August 4, 1943 when 53% completed; completed December 4, 1943

YRD(H)–4 workshop, floating dry dock (hull), keel laid August 16, 1943, launched September 20, 1943

YRD(M)–4 workshop, floating dry dock (machinery), keel laid August 17, 1943, launched September 20, 1943

BREEMAN—DE–104 escort vessel, 1240 tons, transferred to NNSY September 8, 1943 when 46% complete; completed December 27, 1943

YRD(H)–5 workshop, floating dry dock (hull), keel laid October 15, 1943, launched October 26, 1943

YRD(M)–5 workshop, floating dry dock (machinery), keel laid October 15, 1943, launched October 26, 1943

TARAWA CV–40, aircraft carrier, 27100 tons, keel laid March 1, 1944, launched May 12, 1945

YF–1092 covered lighter (self propelled), keel laid January 14, 1946, launched March 15, 1946

BOLD AM–424, minesweeper, wood (non-metallic), 665 tons, keel laid December 12, 1951, christened March 28, 1953

BULWARK AM–425, minesweeper, wood (non-metallic), 665 tons, keel laid December 12, 1951, christened March 28, 1953

Appendix C

DRY DOCKS
Norfolk Naval Shipyard
Portsmouth, Virginia

DRYDOCK NO.	LENGTH	COMMENCED	OPENED
1	319'5"	1 December 1827	17 June 1833
2	498'6"	November 1887	19 September 1889
3	550'	30 November 1903	8 December 1908
4	1011'10"	8 January 1917	1 April 1919
5*			
6	465'9"	6 February 1919	31 October 1919
7	465'8"	17 October 1918	31 October 1919
8	1092'5"	July 1940	July 1942

*Never built, the space was used for other purposes.

APPENDIX D

R U L E S
For the Regulation of the Navy-Yard at Gosport

It being essential to the Public Interest, that the Officers, Workmen, and others employed in the Service of the United States, at the Navy Yard at Gosport, should conduct themselves with Order and Regularity in the execution of their several Duties, whereby the same may be carried on with Economy and Dispatch—I HEREBY ORDER AND DIRECT, that all Officers, Workmen, and others of every denomination whatsoever, employed therein, do conform themselves to the following REGULATIONS as a GENERAL RULE for their conduct.

O F F I C E R S

Each officer will receive from the Constructor, such Orders and Instructions, from time to time, as may be judged best for the Public Service, to which he must undeviatingly adhere: He will have such persons placed under his directions as may be deemed necessary: he will direct them in the performance of such parts of the work as he may be entrusted with, which will be his duty to forward by all means in his power, and see that the same be properly and efficiently executed, at the smallest expense possible.

He will discourage those placed under his direction, from quarrelling, committing excesses of any kind, or absenting themselves from work. He will use his utmost endeavors to protect all public property placed under his charge, or otherwise disposed. It is expected, that he shall attend to the business of the Navy Yard in Preference to any other whatever, and shall on no account absent himself therefrom, without leave, except in case of sickness, or other unavoidable causes. He will be careful to check each person under his direction, for the time he may be absent from his work: and observe those who show an idle disposition: and in all cases to report transgressors.

ARTIFICERS, LABOURERS, &c. &c.

All persons on being entered in the Navy Yard, will report their real names to the Constructor and Clerk, that they may be inserted in the roll.

Such wages will be allowed to each Workman or other person, as the Constructor may judge his qualifications entitle him to receive, which shall be paid on the Saturday of each week, (or as soon after as can be done) to himself, or the person who may be qualified to receive the same, as circumstances may be.

To each Workman who may be sent on board any ship or vessel to work, the same lying below Fort Norfolk, one quarter of a dollar per day, will be allowed him in addition to his Wages at the Yard: to those who may work on board any ship or vessel above that place, the same wages will be paid him, as if he had actually worked in the yard, and no more.

As soon as possible after his name has been entered on the roll, he will be placed under the direction of a Quarterman, or other Officer, as occasion may require, to whom he will apply for instructions respecting his work, &c. and from whose orders he shall in no wise deviate, (unless directed so to do by a Superior Officer) but in all respects he is to execute the same with diligence, care, fidelity, economy and dispatch.

The time of Daily Labour will be from sun-rise to sun-set: The commencement and termination of which will be noticed by Ringing of the Yard-Bell, as well as at Breakfast and Dinner: for the former three quarters of an hour in Winter, and one Hour in Summer will be allowed; for the latter, one Hour in Winter and two in Summer: The Winter to be considered from the first of September to the first of May; and the Summer from the first of May to the first of September following. N. B. From Sun-rise to Noon is to be understood as comprising one half a Day's Work; and from Noon to Sun-set the remaining half—and he shall not at any time quit his work, before the Bell rings for that purpose, without leave of his Officer, unless compelled thereto by rain or other unavoidable cause.

To perform his work in the best and most expeditious manner, he shall provide himself with such Tools as the officer placed over him may deem required for his occupation,—He shall not make use of Tools belonging to another person, without his leave, neither shall he conceal, injure, nor destroy them.

He shall not loiter at his work, nor set an example of idleness to others by unnecessary conversations or otherways—He shall neither Game, Quarrel, give abusive Language, get intoxicated, or insult any Person whatsoever within the Yard, nor be absent on Public Day.

He is not to perform work for individuals during the hours of Work, without leave being first obtained; and it will be expected that he shall not leave his Work to perform Military Duty without leave (except in the case of an emergency) unless the Fine for absence shall exceed the amount of a Day's Work.

He shall not willfully Waste, Destroy, nor embezzle any part of the Public Property, nor suffer others to do it; and it is strictly forbidden to cut up any serviceable Timber, Boards, &c. for Chips—He is not to break the Fence of the Yard, or enclosures, nor take off any Boards. &c. from the same, nor suffer others to do it, without leave being first obtained from the principle Officer at the time in the Yard.

In case of fire happening in the Yard, or to any Ship of War, or other Public Vessel lying in the vicinity thereof, it will be required of him to use every endeavor in his powers to extinguish the flame, and preserve and protect all Public property that may in any wise be endangered thereby—And it is strictly ordered that no fires shall be kindled in the Yard, but at such places as may be appointed for that purpose.

He will be accountable for such Tools, Implements, &c. belonging to the United States, as he may occasionally be furnished with, and in case they are left or willfully destroyed, the amount of their value will be deducted from his wages.

If any person finds himself insulted, or personally aggrieved, he is required to make his case known to the Constructor, on in his absence to the Superior Officer, who will take the same into consideration, and afford him such redress as circumstances may dictate.

As it may happen that Workmen and others, whose residence is distant from the Yard, may have occasion to quit their Work on Saturday Afternoons at an early hour, those will have the time noticed, and when the same shall amount to a Day's Work, it will be deducted from their wages.

A printed copy of the preceding "Rules for the Regulation of the Navy Yard:" shall be hung up in the CLERK's OFFICE. Or some other conspicuous place, for the perusal of all Persons concerned; and no plea will be admitted of ignorance of any part thereof.

Given under my hand at the Navy Yard, Gosport, this_____day of_____, 18____

JOSIAH FOX, Navy Constructor and Superintendent.

INDEX

Adams, George F. 98
ADDER, USS 95, 96
Admiral's Row 101
Aegis-class 125
ALABAMA, USS 100, 119, 120
ALBERT 20
Alexander II, Czar 83
Alexis, Grand Duke 83
Algiers 35
Algiers, Regency of 23
ALLEGHENY, USS 69
Allen Shipyard 72
ALLIANCE, USS 83
American Chain Company 108
American navy 1, 26, 59, 84, 111
American Sea Songs and Chanteys 5
Anderson, Major 63
Annapolis, Maryland 49, 53, 95
Antarctica 67, 68
ARCHER, HMS 115
Argentina 104
ARIZONA, USS 111
ARLEIGH BURKE, USS 125
Armed Forces Staff College 121
Armored Yacht, the 92
Arsenal of Democracy 115
Atlantic Fleet
    97, 103, 114, 118, 121, 122, 125
Atlantic Hotel 83
Atlantic Iron Works 67
Atlantic Ocean 1, 3, 85, 86, 103
Atlantic Squadron
    52, 61, 85, 91, 92, 113
AUK, USS 120
Axis 103, 116
BAGLEY, USS 120
Bagnall, Anthony 2
Bainbridge, William 25, 27, 31, 55
Baker Brothers Salvage Company 75
Baldwin, Laomni 55
Baltimore, Maryland 25, 41
Bancroft Hall 49
Barbary -pirates 35
BARBER, USS 120
Barbour, James 55
Barron, James (Commodore) 31
Barron, James 11
Barron, James (born 1768) 53
Barron, James (Commodore) 26–33,
    35

Barron, Richard 14, 15, 17
Barron, Samuel 27, 53
Base Force 114
Battle of the Capes 16
battleship modernization 111, 112
Beacon, the 71
Beaman, Nathaniel 98
BEAUFORT, USS 76
Belgium 107
"Ben Block" 46
BEN FRANKLIN, USS 72
Berkley 1
Berkley, Admiral 29
Bermuda 14, 117
Bermuda Station 19
BIRMINGHAM, USS 109
Black Hawk, Chief 59, 60
Black Hole 20
Black-beard 35
Bladensburg, Maryland 26, 32
BLUE, USS 120
Board of Commissioners 9
BONHOMME RICHARD 20, 21
Booth, William 11
Boston, Massachusetts 23, 33, 56, 79
Bourne, William T. 63, 64
Boutakoff, Rear Admiral 84
British blockade 11, 13, 14
British navy 3, 10, 11, 19, 29, 35
British-American Tobacco 108
Brodie, Charles D. 48
BROOKLYN, USS 91
Buchanan, Franklin 53, 77–78
Bureau of Yards and Docks 106–107
Burton, H. W. "Scratch" 84
Bush, A. J. 115
Byrd, William 4
Calvert, Thomas 26
Campbell, Hugh 31
Cape Charles 29, 117
Cape Francis 15
Cape Hatteras 81, 116
Cape Henry 1, 11–15, 25, 28–29,
    86, 117
Cape Lookout 116
Cassin, John 47, 48
Cedar Grove Cemetery 37
Cervera, Admiral 92
Charleston, South Carolina 92
Charlestown shipyard 56

CHASE, USS 120
Chauncey, Issac 31
Chesapeake and Ohio 89
Chesapeake Bay
  1, 15, 59, 92, 109, 117–118
CHESAPEAKE, USS 24–26, 28–33,
  35, 41, 90, 125
Chevalier, Godfrey 111
Civil War 11, 40, 48–49, 56–57,
  73, 80–81, 85, 87, 89, 90, 122
Clark, Miss 45
CLEASJE, HNMS 115
Coast Squadron 92
Cockburn, George 42–43
Cocke, William H. 36–37, 39
Cold War 120, 122
Colley 4
COLON 92
COLUMBIA, USS 73
Columbian Exposition 83, 85, 97
Columbian Naval Rendezvous 85, 88
Columbus, Christopher 85, 87–88
COLUMBUS, USS 73
Committees of Correspondence 9
Comte de Grasse, Admiral 14, 15
CONCORDE, USS 15
Confederate States of America 73
CONGRESS, USS 24–25, 74, 76–78
CONNECTICUT, USS 100
Constantine, Grand Duke 83
CONSTELLATION, USS 24–25, 42,
  62, 72, 125
CONSTITUTION, USS 24–25, 28,
  41, 68–69, 72, 125
Cornwallis 14, 15, 16
County Wharf 57
Court of Honor 99
Covered Wagon 111. *See also*
  LANGLEY, USS
Cox, John 13–14
Craney Island 12–13, 41–43, 81,
  118, 122
CRAVEN (DD–70), USS 107
Creighton, J. Blakeley 84
Crowell, Benedict 110
Cuba 37, 91, 121
Cuffee 14
CUMBERLAND, USS 73–78
Dahlgren, John 53
DAKOTA, USS 81
Dale, Richard 17–21
Dale, Winfield 19
Dam Neck training center 120
Daniels, Josephus 101

DAYTONIAN, HMS 115
Decatur, Stephen 26–28, 31–32, 53
DECOY, USS 36
DELAWARE, USS 40, 45–49,
  57, 60–61, 73
Denmark 104
Desert Shield/Desert Storm 122
Dewey, George 92
Discovery Landing 99
Dismal Swamp Canal 52
DOLPHIN, USS 73
Douglas, John Erskine 29
DOWNES, USS 120
DRAGON 11
Drewry's Bluff 74
Drum Beat 116
Dry Dock I 57, 60, 75, 81, 90
Dry Dock IV 106, 107
Dry Dock VI 107
Dry Dock VII 107
Dupont de Nemours, E. I. 108
Dyson Shipyard 67
EAGLE 14
Eagle Iron Works 67
Earl of Dunmore 7. *See also* Murray, John
Eckenrode, H. J. 8
Edmonds, M. B. 114
Eilbeck 4
Eitel Wilhelm 106
Elizabeth River 1–3, 7, 10–15, 19,
  21, 25, 28, 36, 39, 41, 46,
  49, 51, 55, 59, 62, 67, 71–72,
  76, 79, 81, 83, 85, 90, 99, 103,
  105–110, 114, 118–121
Ely, Eugene 109
Emmerson, Arthur 42
England 8, 34, 89
English Channel 20
Ericsson, John 52, 76, 79
ESSEX, USS 35, 39
Evans, Robley "Fighting Bob" 100
Evans, Samuel 32, 33
Farragut, David Glasgow 39–40, 53,
  122
FECHTELER, USS 120
Fifth Naval District 114, 116
Fillmore, Millard 69
First Street Gate 61
Florida 37
FLYING FISH, USS 68
FORMIDABLE, HMS 115
Forrest, French 74
Fort Monroe 59–60, 73–74, 81,
  84, 87

Fort Norfolk 42, 62, 75, 119
Fort Wool 87
Fox, Josiah 24
FOX, USS 36, 37
FRANKFURT 109
freedom of the seas 1, 24, 29, 32, 125
Freemason Street 82
French West Indies 14
Funda Bay 36
GALENA, USS 83
Gatling gun 84
GENERAL ADMIRAL 87
general quarters 29, 30
GEORGE WASHINGTON, USS 125
Georgia 23
GEORGIA, USS 100
GERM 52
GERMANTOWN, USS 73
Germany 89, 101, 104
Gherardi, Bancroft 86–88
"Glory and Pride of the World" 45
Goldsborough, L. M. 81
Gordon, Captain 30
Gosport, England 8
Gosport shipyard 3, 7, 9, 10, 17,
    21–27, 33–41, 45–48, 51–53,
    56, 59, 61–64, 67, 68, 71–76,
    80, 81
Granby Street 108, 118
Grande Island 92
"Grapple" 46
Graves, Thomas 15, 16
Graveyard of the Atlantic 95
Great Bridge 8
Great White Fleet 85, 97, 99, 100
Greene, Dana 80
Greenpoint, New York 76
Green's Iron Works 67
Grice 4
Grice, Francis 57
Griffin, Virgil C. 111
Guadaloupe 25
GUERRIERE, USS 47, 53
HALIFAX, HMS 32
Halifax, Novia Scotia 33
Halsey Field House 49
Hammerhead Crane 115
Hampton Boulevard
    99, 104, 118, 121
Hampton Roads Naval Operating Base 101
Hampton Roads Naval Rendezvous
    Association 86
Hampton Roads, Virginia
    1, 3, 10, 12, 33, 35,

Hampton Roads (continued)
    39, 41, 46, 55, 56, 59, 62,
    67–79, 83–92, 97, 98, 99, 100,
    103, 104, 109, 113, 116, 121, 125
Hampton, Virginia 26, 77, 87, 122
Harrington, Purnell 95
Harrison, Benjamin 86
HARRY S. TRUMAN, USS 125
HARTFORD, USS 40, 84, 122
Haviland, John 55
HELM, USS 120
Henry, Patrick 13
Herbert 4
Herbert, John 10
HERNDON, USS 120
Hogge, Shirley 119
HOPPING, USS 120
HULBERT (DD-342), USS 107
Hull, Isaac 31
Humphreys, Salisbury Price 29, 30, 33
Hunter, William H. 51, 52
Hutchings, John 9
IDAHO, USS 111
ILLINOIS, USS 100
ILLUSTRIOUS, HMS 114, 115
impressment 24
Independence Hall 101
INDOMITABLE, HMS 115
INFANTE MARIA TERESA 91
International Columbian Naval
    Rendezvous 85, 88
INTREPID 27
IOWA, USS 121, 122
Iraq 122
isolationists 23, 24
Jackson, Andrew 59
Jacobs, Randall 113
James I 2
James River 1, 2, 74, 80
Jamestown Exposition Company 97
Jamestown, Virginia
    2, 85, 97, 98, 101
Japan 67, 69, 73, 89, 100, 111
JEFFERSON CITY, USS 125
Jefferson, Thomas 11, 14, 15
Jones, Catesby A. P. 78
Jones, Jacob 31
Jones, John Paul 20, 21
"Junius Brutus Stump" 46
JUPITER, USS 110
KANSAS, USS 100
KEARSAGE, USS 100
KENTUCKY, USS 100, 120, 121
Key West, Florida 37

Index

Kidd, William 35
Kill Devil Hills, North Carolina 95
King, Earnest J. 113, 114
Kitty Hawk, North Carolina 95
Korean War 121
KRASSIN 115
KRONPRINZ WILHELM 105
LADY SUSAN 19
LAKE CHAMPLAIN, USS 120
Langley, Samuel Pierpont 110
LANGLEY, USS 110, 111
LANING, USS 120
"Launch" 45
Lawrence, James 31, 33
Lee, Fitzhugh 97, 98
Lee, Robert E. 98
Lend-Lease 116
LEOPARD, HMS 28–30, 32, 41
LEXINGTON 19, 20
LIBERTY 10
Lincoln, Abraham 75, 81
Linde Air Products 108
Linton, Captain 63
Little Creek 12, 118
Little Creek Amphibious Base 3
live oak 24
LOUISIANA, USS 100
LOVELACE, USS 120
Lowenberg, M. D. 98
LOY, USS 120
Loyall, Paul 10
LSD 118
LST 118
Luke, William Benson 49
LUSITANIA 106
Lynnhaven, Virginia 12
MACEDONIA, USS 68
MACEDONIAN, USS 69
Madagascar 68
Mahaffey's Iron Works 67
MAINE, USS 89, 100
Malta, Battle of 115
manifest destiny 89
Manila, Philipines 92
Marchant, Susan Caroline 40
Mare Island 110
Mariners' Museum 81
Martin 32
Martin-type bombers 110
Mason, George 16
Maury, Matthew Fontaine 53
Maxwell, James 10
MAYFLOWER 99
McAlphine, Chief Engineer 91

McCauley, Charles S. 74
McLean, Walter 106
MERRIMAC(K), USS 57, 73–80, 90
Mexican War 69
Mill Prison 20
MINNESOTA, USS 74–79, 100
Minor, Lewis 56
"Minute Gun at Sea" 46
MISSISSIPPI, USS 69, 111, 121
MISSOURI, USS 100, 121, 122
Mitchell, Billy 109, 110
MOCCASIN, USS 95, 96
MOLLY 10, 12, 13
MONITOR, USS 56, 76–81, 86, 87
MONITOR-MERRIMAC Memorial
    Bridge Tunnel 80
Monroe, Fort 73
Morgan, John T. 23
Moro Castle 37
Morris 55
Morris, Charles 28
Morris, Christopher 11–13
MORRIS, USS 120
Mosquito Fleet 36, 39
MOUNT VERNON, USS 81
Murray, Alexander 31
Murray, John 7
Myers, Moses 4
Nash and Herbert shipyard 25
Nash, Thomas 10, 25, 67
National Defense University System
    121
National Expedition to the Southern
    Ocean 68
National Industrial Recovery Act 112
Naval Amphibious Base 118
Naval Construction Act of 1794 23
naval hospital
    55, 56, 61, 86, 88, 92, 105, 121
Naval Institute Proceedings 111
Neilson, Adelaide 83
NEVADA, USS 104, 111
NEW JERSEY, USS 100, 121
New Orleans, Battle of 41
New York
    15, 16, 64, 76, 79, 83, 85, 88
NEW YORK, USS 73, 91, 111
New York World's Fair 113
Newport News, Virginia
    74, 76, 80, 81, 89, 98
Newport, Rhode Island 95
Newton 4
Newton, Josiah 19, 21
Newton, Thomas, Jr. 9

NINA 88
NOA (DD-343), USS 107
NORFOLK (brig) 25, 26
Norfolk and Western 89
Norfolk County 8, 19, 64
Norfolk Herald 24, 48, 56, 63
Norfolk International Terminal 105
Norfolk Naval Air Station 117
Norfolk Naval Base
    3, 97, 103, 105, 106, 112,
    117–122, 125
Norfolk Naval Shipyard
    1, 3, 23, 61, 81, 83, 89, 92, 95,
    96, 99, 103–115, 118, 119, 121
Norfolk plan 106
Norfolk Shipbuilding and Dry Dock
    Company 108
Norfolk Shipbuilding and Drydock
    Company 119
NORFOLK, SSN 25
Norfolk, Virginia
    1, 2, 3, 4, 8, 9, 12, 15–17,
    24, 26, 31, 32, 39, 42, 45, 65, 67,
    72–75, 78–89, 99, 103, 104,
    108–122, 125
Norfolk Virginian 86
Norfolk: Historic Southern Port 98
North Carolina 35, 74, 95, 116
NORTH CAROLINA (BB-52), USS
    108
Norway 104
Nova Scotia 30, 33
Obolinski, Prince 84
Ocean View 81, 118
Oceana Naval Air Station 120
OHIO, USS 100
Old Ironsides 67
Old Point Comfort 2, 12, 86
Onslow Bay 116
Operation Torch 118
OQUENDO 91, 92
OREGON, USS 68, 91, 92
OSPREY, USS 120
OSTFRIESLAND 109, 110
Outer Banks, North Carolina
    35, 74, 95
Page and Allen Shipyard 67, 72
Page shipyard 67
Panama Canal 110
PATRIOT 15
PAWNEE, USS 74
PEACOCK, USS 36, 68
Pearl Harbor, Hawaii 73, 116
Pegram, Robert 74

Pennock, William 24
PENNSYLVANIA, USS 53, 73
PEORIA, USS 95
Percival, John "Madjack" 68
Perry, Matthew Calbraith 69
Perry, Oliver Hazard 69
Perry Voyage 67
PHILADELPHIA, USS 27, 28, 86, 87
Philipines 92
Phillip, John W. 91, 92
Pierce, Franklin 71
PINTA 88
PIONEER, USS 68
PIRATES 36
pirates 4, 27, 35, 36, 37, 40
Pittsburgh shipyard 75
Plymouth, England 20
PLYMOUTH, USS 69, 73
Point L'Orient, France 20
PORPOISE, USS 37, 69
Porter 4, 67
Porter, David 31
Porter, David W. 36, 37, 39
Porter, John L. 72, 75, 76, 80
Porter shipyard 67
Portsmouth, England 8, 34
Portsmouth Naval Hospital 117
Portsmouth Naval Shipyard Museum
    52, 122
Portsmouth, Virginia 1, 2, 4, 12–16,
    24, 32, 33, 37, 42, 43, 45, 65, 67,
    72–74, 80, 84, 89, 92, 97–123,
    125
POTOMAC 114
Potomac River 79
Potter, Edward E. 87
POWHATAN, USS 69
Preble, Edward 27
PRESIDENT, USS 24, 25, 35
PRINCE EITEL FREDERICK 105
PRINCETON, USS 69
Puerto Rico 37
pumps 107
Quasi-War 25, 27
Raleigh Square 99
RALEIGH, USS 76, 86, 90, 92
RARITAN, USS 73
Ratford, Jenkins 32
RAVEN, USS 120
red cedar 24
REEVES, USS 120
REINA MERCEDES 91
RELIEF, USS 68
RENOWN 14

REUBEN JAMES, USS 120
Revolution in Virginia, The 8
Revolutionary War 4, 10, 29, 45
Rhinehart, Joseph Cooper 68
Rhode Island 95
RHODE ISLAND, USS 100
Rip Raps 13
ROANOKE, USS 76, 77
Rodger, John 31
Romanovs 83
Romeo and Juliet 83
Roosevelt, Franklin Delano 112–115
Roosevelt, Theodore 91, 92, 99, 100
Rosie the Riveter 119
Rough Riders 91
Rowan, Stephen C. 49
ROWAN, USS 120
ROYAL SOVEREIGN, HMS 115
Saint Helena 104, 118, 122
SALLY MORTON, USS 13
SALLY, USS 10, 12
Sampson, William T. 92
SAN JACINTO, USS 81
San Juan, Puerto Rico 37
SANTA MARIA 85, 88
Santiago Harbor, Cuba 91
SARANAC, USS 71
SARATOGA, USS 69
Schley, Winfield Scott 91
Schmoele tract 106
SEA GULL 36
SEMINOLE, USS 81
SERAPIS, HMS 20, 21
Sewell's Point 1–3, 13, 14, 74, 79,
    86, 89, 97, 98, 100, 103–105,
    117
SHANGRI-LA, USS 120
SHANNON, HMS 33
SHARK 36
Shaw, John 31
Shawl Dance 45
Shay, Frank 5
Shilling, Baron 84
Shiskin, Baron 83
Shoemaker, Charles F. 62, 63
SHUBRICK, USS 120
Shubrick, William B. 51
SIMS, USS 120
Singleton, Henry 56
"Skyscraper" 46
Smith, Constantine 63, 64
Smith, John 2
Smithsonian Institution 68
"Song of the Origin of Gunpowder" 46

Southard, Samuel 55
Spain 85, 89, 90
Spanish American War 98
Speed the Plough 45
Spiller, William 45
"Spritsail" 46
Sprowle, Andrew 3, 4, 7, 9, 10
St. Croix 14
St. Eustatia 14
St. Helena 47, 56
ST. LAWRENCE, USS 76, 77
STACK, USS 120
Standard Oil 108
Stanton, Edwin 79
Stcherbatov, Prince Nicolas 84
steam engine 51, 52
STEVENS, USS 81
Stewart, William H. 85, 88
Stoddart, Benjamin 24
Stodder, David 10
Strachan 32
Strakosch, Max 83
Stuart, Elizabeth 2
"Studding Sail" 46
Subic Bay 92
Supreme Allied Command, Atlantic
    121
SUSQUEHANNA, USS 69
Sweden 104
SWETLANA 84
Tamenend 49, 60
TARAWA, USS 120
Tarbell, Joseph 31
Taussig, J.K. 114
Taylor, Alfred "Red" 115
Tazewell, Littleton 31
Teach, Edward 35
Tecumseh 49
TEXAS, USS 86, 90–92, 111, 113
THEODORE ROOSEVELT, USS 125
Thomas, Henry George 69
Thomas Shipyard 67
Tokyo, Japan 69
"Tom Starboard" 46
Torpedo Junction 117
Tortola 14
Tory 8
Tracy, Benjamin F. 86
Travis, Champion 9
Tredegar Iron Works 75
Tripoli 27, 28, 35
Trophy Park 23, 61
TRUMBULL, USS 21
TUCKER, USS 120

Index

Tucker, William 3
Turon 68
U-boat 92, 116–118
UNION, USS 52
United States Army Base 104
United States Life Saving Station 96
United States Marine Corp 63
United States Marines 62
United States Naval Academy
    49, 53, 77
United States Navy 1, 4, 9, 11, 21,
    27, 45, 69, 75, 82, 84, 85, 89,
    90, 99, 100, 108, 118, 120
UNITED STATES, USS
    24, 25, 27, 73
VAINQUELRE 25
Van Buren, Martin 68
VERMONT, USS 69, 100
Vietnam 68, 122
VINCENNES, USS 68, 69
Virginia Assembly 11
Virginia Capes 1, 41, 95, 117
Virginia capes 74
Virginia Coal and Navigation 108
Virginia, colonial 1
Virginia Colonial Navy 9
Virginia Company 3
Virginia Convention 9
VIRGINIA, CSS 56, 57, 76–82,
    85, 87, 90
Virginia Navy 11–19, 26
Virginia Pilots Association 82
VIRGINIA, USS 100
Virginian (Norfolk) 87
Virginian Railroad 89
Virginian-Pilot 104
Virginia's Golden Leaf 3
Volunteer Corps 47
WAHTAH, USS 120
WAINWRIGHT, USS 120
War of 1812
    11, 26, 32, 39, 40, 41, 45, 51, 69
Ware 32
WARREN, USS 27
Warrington, Lewis 40, 48, 53, 55, 57
WASHINGTON 51
Washington, George 11, 14, 15, 16
Washington Naval Limitation Treaty
    108
WASP, USS 125
WATER WITCH, USS 71
Wayne, Thomas S. 62, 63
Webb, George 9

Weinberger, Caspar 25
Wertenbaker, Thomas Jefferson
    98, 103
Wheeler, Susan 28
White, Joseph 14
Whiting, Paul 111
Whiting, Thomas 9
Wickham, England 34
Wilkes, Charles 68
Wilkes Expedition 67
Wilkes Land 68
WILLIAM B. PRESTON (DD-344),
    USS 107
WILLIAM GRAVES 14
Williams, Hezekiah 78
Williams, Thomas 25
Williamsburg, Virginia 3, 13, 14, 15
Williamson, Dr. William P. 55
Williamson, William P. 55
Williamson, William P., (engineer) 75
Willoughby Spit 1, 12, 29
Wilson, Woodrow 101, 103
WISCONSIN, USS 107, 121, 122
Wise, Nicholas, Jr. 3
Wood, J.T. 98
Wood, John 3
Wool, James E. 81
World War I 89, 97, 101, 103,
    106–111, 117, 118
World War II 89, 111, 118–121
Worthington centrifugal pumps 107
Wright brothers 95, 96
WYOMING, USS 114
YANKTIC 95
Yedo Bay, Tokyo 69
yellow fever 55, 68, 72, 73
yeomanettes 105
York River 1, 16
Yorktown, Virginia 14–16, 85

ABOUT THE AUTHOR

A Portsmouth, Virginia native, Alan Flanders was educated at Old Dominion University, George Washington University, Hollins College and Oxford University. He holds degrees in English and history, including a Ph.D. specializing in naval history. He is currently a Research Fellow with Queen Elizabeth House and a member of the middle common room, St. Edmund Hall, Oxford University.

For the past fifteen years, Flanders's feature stories on Hampton Roads history have appeared in the *Virginian-Pilot's* "Olde Towne Journal." His articles have also appeared in *Naval Institute Proceedings, American Heritage, American History Illustrated,* and *Civil War Times.*

He has written four other books on naval history, including *Around the World in Old Ironsides: The Voyage of USS* Constitution, *1844–1846; E.A. Jack, Confederate Steam Engineer on CSS* Virginia; and *Guardians of the Capes: A History of Pilots and Piloting in Virginia Waters from 1611 to the Present.*

Flanders is past president of the board of the Norfolk Historical Society, a board member of the Portsmouth Historical Association and former board member of the Armed Forces YMCA and the Navy League of Hampton Roads.